the GREEN WICCAN book of HERBS

Dedication

I'd like to thank my mother, who was a wonderful teacher in the mysteries of nature, and kept me supplied with fresh and dried herbs from her own garden while I was living in a small apartment in Dublin; some of the recipes in Chapter 7 are things I have adapted from what she taught me. This book is for you!

the GREEN WICCAN book of HERBS

your complete guide to herbal magic

Silja

CICO BOOKS

This edition published in 2026 by CICO Books
an imprint of Ryland Peters & Small Ltd
20–21 Jockey's Fields
London WC1R 4BW
www.rylandpeters.com
Email: euregulations@rylandpeters.com

First published in 2009 as
The Green Wiccan Herbal

10 9 8 7 6 5 4 3 2 1

A CIP record for this book is available from the British Library.
US Library of Congress CIP data has been applied for.

ISBN: 978-1-80065-668-0

Printed in China

Designer: Roger Hammond,
bluegumdesigners.com
Illustrator: Michael A. Hill

MIX
Paper | Supporting responsible forestry
FSC® C106563
FSC
www.fsc.org

Cover designer: Emily Breen
Production manager: Gordana Simakovic

The authorised representative in the EEA is
Authorised Rep Compliance Ltd.,
Ground Floor, 71 Lower Baggot Street,
Dublin, D01 P593, Ireland
www.arccompliance.com

SAFETY NOTES

Neither the author nor the publisher can be held responsible for any claim arising out of the general information and practices provided in this book. While the use of essential oils, herbs, incense, and particular practices refer to healing benefits, they are not intended to replace diagnosis of illness or ailments, or healing or medicine. Always consult your doctor or other health professional in the case of illness. Some plants are poisonous. Do not touch or ingest any part of a plant unless you are sure it is safe to do so, and keep them away from pets and children. It is the sole responsibility of the reader to correctly identify a plant before working with it. Seek advice from a qualified professional if unsure. Essential oils are very powerful and potentially toxic if used too liberally. Follow the advice given on the label and never use the oils neat on bare skin, or if pregnant without consulting a health professional. The safe and proper use of candles and incense is the sole responsibility of the person using them. Never burn a flame on or near anything that might catch fire and do not leave unattended. Keep out of the reach of children and pets and ensure good ventilation.

CONTENTS

Introduction 6

Chapter 1
The Basics of Herbal magic 9

Chapter 2
Herbal History and Mythology 20

Chapter 3
Growing and Storing Magical Herbs 29

Chapter 4
The 52 Major Magical Herbs 48

Chapter 5
Other Foods and their Magical Uses 76

Chapter 6
Herbal Spells 86

Chapter 7
Magical Herbs: Kitchen Witchery 124

Chapter 8
How to Write your own Magical Spells 144

Tables of Magical Associations 154

Glossary 156

Resources 157

Index 158

Introduction

This Herbal was a joy to write, as I love herbs and find them so useful in both my work as a witch and as a housewife and mother, so I was glad to be able to pass on some of my knowledge about these little power plants.

I can't really pinpoint a time when I became interested in herbs. I think it's almost part of my blood, as well as my upbringing; when I was little, my parents both worked from home and we had a big garden where my mother would grow veggies and herbs for cooking, as we weren't exactly rich at the time. I had my own little garden too, and while I mostly grew flowers as a little girl, I was always partial to the mint family of herbs, especially peppermint (it makes such a refreshing tea!) and citronella (to keep away the bugs on balmy summer nights spent outdoors). Not only did growing our own herbs and other foods save money, but it also meant we were able to live in tune with nature, eating seasonal foods and healing minor ailments with herbal teas my mother made by drying garden herbs or with those we gathered on long walks in the countryside.

I've never been one for hot spicy foods, much to my husband's disappointment, but I do love flavorsome herbs in cooking, and I think I got that from childhood. Even a boring piece of bread and butter or a plain yogurt can be made into something special, and magical, by adding some herbs. I learnt this from my mother, who is the first kitchen witch I came across—although she does not call herself that and is not a Wiccan by religion, just a wise women in tune with everything around her. Later, I moved to Dublin to go to college, where I lived in a one-bedroom apartment with little space to grow anything! Between lack of space and keeping up to four cats (they were rescue animals and I had a hard time saying no...) growing my own herbs was difficult. However, I had a steady supply from my

CHINESE PROVERB

"Better a dinner of herbs than a stalled ox where hate is."

mother and, once I really got into Wicca, my coven members and I would often go for walks in the countryside to do rituals in secluded spots, gathering some herbs and sacred plants on the way. Magical herbs often featured during the rituals on Sabbat nights as well as in the potluck dinners afterward! Still, I was very glad when I was able to move to a lovely house with a big garden with my family, and I can now grow my own magical herbs again, teach my kids about Mother Nature, and even have space enough to experiment. This year, I am arranging some raised stone beds to see if the enhanced drainage and warmer soil will improve the way my herbs grow.

A book always has some limitations as to what information you can cover—each of the chapters following this introduction could easily be expanded into their own book: there is so much information about magical herbs, how to grow them, and their mythology, and I could fill several volumes with all the spells I have! But I trust I have achieved a good balance of information about herbs here, and not just imparted some of my knowledge, but also encouraged you to expand your own and develop your witchy skills and intuition, and your closeness to nature. I hope you enjoy reading this book as much as I have enjoyed writing it!

"Lavender is for lovers true,
Which evermore be faine;
Desiring always for to have
Some pleasure for their paine:
And when that they obtained have
The love that they require
Then have they all their perfect joie
And quenched is the fire."
Clement Robinson

CHAPTER 1

The Basics of Herbal Magic

To be able to use herbs magically, you need to know how magic works, so you can enjoy discovering the magical energy of the plants.

This chapter will give you the basics you need to make the most out of the rest of the book, and help you learn how to use herbs in basic magic.

Magical Theory: Why and How Magic Works

I'll start off with the bad news: magic doesn't always work. Because magic only changes probability, it means you won't be 100 percent successful, even if you're an experienced witch. For example, if you do a spell to win the lottery, even if your chances double, the percentage chance of winning is still tiny. But if you are one of three people up for a promotion and you do a spell to get the job, then doubling your chances means you have a very good shot at that promotion! Magic essentially works with the energy of the universe to change probability; the herbs, colors, and crystals, for example, help with that as they have their own magical energies, but you are the main element. So if a spell does not work, take a close look at all aspects of it: did you do it for the right reasons, or was your intention selfish? Was the herb you used healthy and potent, or was it moldy or weak in magical energy because it grew near the highway and was poisoned by the fumes? Maybe you need to change the colors of the candles you used, or add to the spell by asking for the blessing of a patron deity for the type of spell you are doing (such as Eros for love, Brigit for motherhood, or Ceres for wisdom). Maybe you were so eager to try the spells in this book that you did too many magics at once, thus spreading your own energy too thin. Also, consider the possibility that the spell may have worked without you realizing it. For example, you may have been closed to the possibility that the milkman could be your new lover; or the spell is actually working, but is taking some time to manifest—if you did a money spell, your bosses may be earmarking you for a promotion without your knowledge.

Keep in mind the Garth Brooks song "Sometimes I Thank the Lord for Unanswered Prayers"—maybe your herbal spell or ritual isn't working not because you did something wrong, but because it is just not right for you to move house or start that new relationship at this time in your life.

Magical ethics (black and white magic)

Wiccans have often been accused of being immoral because, unlike most of the world's major religions, Wiccans don't believe that the body or the earth is evil or sinful. In a famous poem-chant, "The Charge of the Goddess," one line says, 'All acts of love and pleasure are my rituals.' Now, you may think that implies we have orgies and have no self-control and just generally give in to whatever urges we have, but that's not what it means. Preparing herbs for magic, cooking food, making music or love, dancing or painting become sacred acts, entered into with a deeper respect and awareness of our personal responsibility, not with looser morals. Wicca doesn't have a Bible or the Ten Commandments, but that doesn't mean it's a religion without values and ethics. Quite the opposite! Wicca has two main ethical guidelines for both doing magic and living spiritually:

1. And it harm none, do what thou wilt

At first glance, this seems pretty easy. But it can be a little more complicated than just making sure that the herb you are going to use isn't poisonous! 'And it harm none' refers not only to other people, but also to yourself, animals, plants, and the Earth herself. We're connected to each other at a variety of levels—spiritually, ecologically, and physically—and we must carefully weigh our actions with their consequences. This is not to mean that we never take action because we're too busy weighing up the consequence of stepping out of the door in the morning, only that our actions should be guided by an awareness of the impact of our deeds. The idea of black versus white magic comes from this moral idea—basically anything that goes against another person's free will or is harmful is considered black magic; beneficial spells would be white magic. However, there is some controversy around this as it isn't really the magic that is black or white, but the intent of the witch performing it.

2. Lest in thy self-defense it be, ever mind the rule of three

This one is a little easier—just think of karma, or as we are talking about gardening here, of reaping what you sow. Wiccans believe that what you do comes back to you threefold, so if you send out bad energy in the form of a spell or action, not only does it backfire on you, but you get three times the consequence. It's important to remember that if you have been harmed by another person's deliberate actions you may not instantly see the consequences in their life, but there will still be repercussions.

Long- versus short-term spells

So, how do you know how long a spell takes to work? Well, this depends mostly on how the spell is written and performed. If a spell has worked, for most magic you will see a result within a lunar cycle, or 28 days, when the moon comes full circle. Also, results show within a lunar cycle because it takes quite a lot of power to make magical energy last longer than this.

Of course, some spells are designed to last longer, especially those for outcomes like home protection or business success spells; but even with these, I recommend renewing the spell every year or so unless you are confident that the magic is still strong. You can give a spell a specific duration, for example a herbal spell to protect a traveler, by actually saying in the spell how long you want it to last or by visualizing the magic being released at a certain time. For example, my "Mustard Seed Spell for Prosperity"

The moon is very important in Wicca, and many magical and coven activities are based on the current moon phase (see Chapter 8, page 149 for a discussion on the moon phases in spells and rituals). Wiccan covens usually meet at or around the full moon for their monthly meetings, called Esbats, and the blue moon (when two full moons happen in one calendar month) is the time that some covens schedule special ceremonies, such as initiations or hand fastings. See also Chapter 3, page 31, on how to harness the moon's magical energy for growing and harvesting your magical herbs.

(Chapter 6, page 89) builds up energy over a waxing moon, and on the full moon the magic is finally released. There are short-term spells, too, such as those designed to promote fun in the bedroom that night or to summon a bus when you are waiting at a wet and windy bus stop; they usually fulfill their magical intent as soon as they are performed and must be renewed every time you want the same result.

Solitary versus coven magic

Many people, when they first become interested in Wicca and witchcraft, are looking to join a coven right away. However, that is the wrong time to join a magical group. Firstly, you should explore Wicca by yourself, both intellectually and spiritually—there are so many different aspects of witchcraft, and so many different traditions and beliefs that it can be difficult to know where to start!
I generally recommend that new witches read a lot, to be exposed to different points of view and practices. I am not saying that joining a coven is a bad thing; I have run one for years. But most established covens are reluctant to take complete newcomers to Wicca, as they are reluctant to share their secrets—and significant hours and effort in training—on someone who in a few months or a year might decide that the tradition of Wicca the coven practices is not for them after all.

Some witches will always work solitary out of choice, so they can do their magic just how they want and do not have to wait for a meeting with others to do a ritual. They will miss out on some group activities, such as guided meditation, the herbal and magical knowledge of others, cooking magical food, and the strong magical energy you can raise in a coven that works well together. The new trend for witches is to do both solitary and group work—they do their serious spell work alone, but meet with other witches socially at moots (witchy meetings held in bars or community centers). There is usually a topic of the month being discussed for an hour or so and then it's just mingling. Witches may also gather to celebrate the main Sabbats (festivals) with others in a semi-public meeting that has arisen from a moot, or with a study group.

Different Types of Spells and Magic

Flower Magic

The fragrant flowers of herbs are used in much of herbalism and spells, but most flower magic is more subtle than that: many people have heard of the Victorians' secret language of flowers, where each flower was given a certain meaning, such as a solid-colored carnation meaning "yes", and a striped one meaning "no". Wicca has adopted this language, but flowers mean even more in witchcraft: simple flowers, such as the wild rose and the apple blossom are used to symbolize the ultimate Wiccan symbol—the pentagram—as their five petals are arranged very much like this shape. As fresh flowers don't keep very long they also symbolize the fleeting nature of magical energy, and that it needs to be handled carefully as it can be easily crushed, just like the petals of a flower.

Flowers are used on the altar to represent the season; in my coven, it is always one coven member's responsibility to bring a bunch of flowers to any Esbat ritual. Preferably, these won't be bought but gathered in the garden or on the way to the ritual, so they are fresh and in season. We try to make the color of the altar flowers suitable for the rituals and spells we intend on working, such as blue corn flowers and violets for wisdom and healing magic, white lilies and fruit tree blossoms for peace rituals, pink roses and tulips for love magic, and yellow daffodils and dandelions for friendship and study spells. Flower magic need not be complicated; if you feel too inexperienced to perform a spell or complicated ritual, why not simply get some edible flowers or a flowering herb and use the colors of the flowers or the magic of the herb to create some gentle magic in the kitchen?

- Fry zucchini (courgette) flowers, thus combining the gold of the batter with the green of the zucchini, to attract money.

- Place some red clover flowers in individual ice-cube trays, add water and freeze to make magical ice cubes that you can add to any drink to attract luck and prosperity, or make a tea with camomile flowers to promote health and inner calm (see the recipe in Chapter 7, page 124).

A new flower suddenly growing in your garden or on your way to work can also be a sign from the deities to pay attention to the corresponding area of your life: if you suddenly notice a yellow buttercup, this may indicate you should pay more attention to friends and the quality of your friendships; if your lawn is overnight blooming with daisies—a symbol of innocence—this may be a sign that you are too naive about a situation or that innocents around you (children, animals) need protecting.

SPELL

The lilac flower is used to ask the blessings of the deities, and the hibiscus is helpful as an aphrodisiac and to induce pleasant dreams. So to ask the blessings of the deities for a new relationship, drop some petals from those flowers into a bath after a first date before you go to bed or have a vase filled with hibiscus and lilac on your bedside table when moving a relationship on to a sexual level.

Candle magic

Many rituals and spells involve the lighting of a few candles, as they give a nice warm light. Candle magic does more than that—it means the candle is center stage in the magic. The simplest type of candle spell is to light a candle and look into the flame, then visualize the goal you want to achieve. You can make this spell more potent by rubbing the candle with a herbal essential oil (such as patchouli for fertility or citronella for happiness), choosing a suitable color (blue for healing, green for prosperity, for example), etching magical symbols (such as a dollar or pound sign for a money spell) into the candle, and/or asking a relevant deity for help (such as Demeter for a work-related spell, or Athena for luck).

If you have difficulty releasing the magical energy after a spell to do its work, candle spells are great because you can blow out the candle gently and watch the smoke disappear, visualizing this as the magical energy going out into the world. Candles are good for longer spells, too, because you can use the same candle for several nights, and it will become more and more magically powerful as time goes on.

Don't use the same candle for different spells, as you do not want to mix different magical energies!

Knot/cord magic

Knot or cord magic is very simple magic, which essentially gathers energy by you tying knots into a length of cord (or appropriately colored ribbon), charging it with magic by saying a chant and then when you are ready, releasing the spell and making it become reality by untying the knots. In some covens, the cord used to tie your magical robe around your waist is used for cord magic; this is especially potent for knot spells because it is constantly worn during coven rituals and when doing magic, so it has soaked up a lot of magical energy. The original knot spell is called a Witches Ladder, and done with a 9-foot (2.75-m) length of cord, with nine knots made while saying the following chant:

"By the knot of one, my spell's begun
By the knot of two, no one can undo
By the knot of three, so may it be
By the knot of four, magic power I store
By the knot of five, this spell's alive
By the knot of six, this spell I fix
By the knot of seven, the blessing is given
By the knot of eight, this is my fate
By the knot of nine, this spell be mine!"

However, it isn't necessary to follow this chant exactly—I rarely use that long a cord, it is just unwieldy, and I like to actually vocalize what I want in the spell, so I change the chant to incorporate what I want (see Chapter 6, page 94, "Pennyroyal Knot Spell for Money and Success" for a money knot spell of my own design). You can also dab some herbal essential oil on each knot to make the magic even stronger. Or, tie some sprigs of an appropriate herb (such as lavender for peace, or chives for breaking bad habits) into the knots to infuse the knot with the magical properties of the herb.

Witch bottles and charm bags

Witch bottles have existed for a very long time; they are a simple way of combining magical ingredients and storing them. Little effort is needed once the ingredients are put together, so it is easy for an experienced witch to make these and then give them to those she wishes to heal or protect, without the "target" needing to do anything. Charm bags are essentially the same thing as witch bottles, except they are little cloth bags, usually of a wisely chosen color. Traditionally, a witch bottle would contain something of the person it was supposed to work on—for example, hair or nail clippings. However, these days, this is generally left out in favor of wearing the bottle as a pendant or keeping a charm bag in your pocket, and therefore close to your body (skin contact is preferred). See Chapter 6, page 113, "Herbal Witch Bottle for Good Health" for a health spell of my own design involving a charm bag.

Dragon and fairy magic

We are not talking about real-fire breathing dragons and knights in shining armor here, but rather spiritual beings or energies from different planes that can sometimes access our plane of existence. Working with dragons and fairies, or spiritual totem animals, can be enlightening as it gives you a different outlook on life and magic (similar to meeting with people from a different culture). You can also ask them to protect you when you do magic and in your day-to-day life.

To attract fairies to your garden, place a glass orb in the middle of some thistles. To attract them to your home, have some faceted crystals hanging in your window, so that they make rainbows onto your walls, or make a little fairy home with matchsticks and place a sugary biscuit and a few juniper berries in the middle.

Dream magic

Dream magic is not so much spell work as fortune-telling. In its simplest form, you lay down to sleep at night and just before drifting off, concentrate on a question you have or a loved one (living or dead) you wish to contact, and then dream of them.

Dreaming can also be used to access other planes of existence in order to talk to spirits and ghosts or meet deities (although think carefully when going to meet deities in dreams—they may not want to be disturbed by a mortal and be grumpy, leading to your magic not working or them playing tricks on you!). There is also an advanced form of dream magic called lucid dreaming—the witch trains herself to be somewhat conscious when asleep and dreaming and thus able to "direct" her dreams and make active decisions within the dream.

Keep a pen and paper by your bed so you can write down any dreams you remember if you wake at night or first thing in the morning—otherwise you are liable to forget. This will also help you access your subconscious more and begin to trust your intuition—a crucial thing for a witch!

You don't need to have an established coven to do magic with friends—they don't even need to be Wiccans! Why not arrange a "herb-swap" party where people who like and/or grow herbs come together and swap herbs for use in the kichen and magic?

Meditations and Visualizations

Witches use meditation for all kinds of things, from raising energy to calming the mind and simply concentrating on tasks and rituals. There are also some more involved forms of meditation, such as guided meditations and vision quests. Guided meditations (when someone else does the talking) are suitable for everyone—meditation CDs are widely available. But many of these CDs do not explain the basics of relaxation, or they move into the actual meditation too quickly. Before you begin to meditate, make sure your body is comfortable and fully relaxed, and your breathing is deep and slow. An intermediate type of meditation is the "happy place"—something that even beginners can do, given enough time. This type of meditation can really help keep you calm and balanced in stressful situations that trigger your emotional responses, such as anger or sadness.

- Start by sitting comfortably or laying down, and close your eyes. Imagine a place in nature that you love—not an actual place you know but a fantasy, an ideal place. For some that may be under a big tree on top of a hill, for some in the middle of a cornfield or at a sandy beach—for me, it's in a forest glade with a babbling stream. Make this place really detailed in your mind—hear the birds singing, feel the moss under your feet, smell the salty air from the sea, and so on. Spend several meditative sessions constructing your happy place. Once you are finished with it, start practicing going there in your mind whenever you have a free moment, such as while waiting for the bus or making a hot drink. Soon, your mind will be able to escape to your happy place easily, and you can go there for a moment's relaxation before that big business meeting, or when your three-year-old is being a pain!

A vision quest is an advanced form of meditation. In covens, this is often practiced as a guided meditation, but that doesn't mean it is easy. If you want to get something out of it, I would recommend a vision quest only when you are comfortable with more basic forms of meditation and have some knowledge of Wiccan spirituality. In a vision quest, you go deep into your subconscious to find out what to do about an issue, or go to meet a deity or spirit to help you with a goal in your life.

Herbs in Rituals

Rituals tend to follow the same pattern, and while it is easier to do a ritual as a coven, you can also perform one by yourself.

Coven ritual

Here is what my coven usually does: we meet up and chat until everyone is there, while I arrange seasonal flowers on the altar and make some magic food to have afterward (sometimes, we go potluck and each coven member will bring food). Then we change into our ritual robes and start the ritual proper by casting the circle:

- Next, we "call the quarters" (the elements) and raise energy. Raising energy doesn't need to be complex, and can give some extra power to any herbal spell or magic: light four candles, for each of the four directions (north, south, east, west), and place them on the ground or on a table/altar. If you like, your candle colors can relate to the elements: brown/green for earth, yellow/white for air, red/orange for fire, and blue for water. Then, ask the elements to attend you, or draw a pentagram in the air with your right hand at each direction.

- Then we call any deities we wish to attend the ritual and play out a piece of mythology or tell a story relevant to the season and our coven. Next, we do the main magic: we perform spells, send out healing, and/or do a guided meditation.

- Once this is done, we relax during what is called the "cakes and ale ceremony" of the Esbat. Traditionally this used to be ale and oat cakes, flavored with a herb appropriate to the season and magic to be done, but now it's basically a fancy name for wine/beer or, in the case of my coven, tea, cookies, and a good chat; the food and drink has a grounding effect after all the power and energy gathered during the ritual. While mundane topics are discussed, we try to keep to spiritual issues, sharing experiences of spells, rituals, and visions. Some of us might discuss new spells we have written and performed, or talk about witchy books we have read.

- We make sure to leave a few crumbs of whatever biscuits we have eaten, and half a cup of tea in the pot. When we are done talking, we gather up the remnants of the food and, with some words of thanks to the deities and spirits, place this by the herbs we may use for magic later in the year, to help them grow. All that remains is to take down the circle we cast by blowing out the candles and incense, and thanking any spirits and deities who were asked to attend (after all, we want to be good hosts not only to our human guests!).

If you already have various herbs collected, why not use herbs for the quarters rather than candles? Use herbs that are strong in their elemental energy, such as garlic for earth, eyebright for air, chili for fire, and camphor for water. This works especially well if you intend to perform herbal magic anyway, or in places where you are not allowed to have open flames, such as in national parks or in dorm rooms.

Chapter 2

Herbal History and Mythology

Wicca relies heavily on the knowledge and wisdom of our ancestors and our culture, and herbalism is a perfect expression of this tradition. Herbs have been used in medicine and spiritual practice since humankind began, and this is reflected in all our culture and mythology, from the tales of Ireland and ancient Greece to Hinduism and Christianity.

Knowing about the history of a herb will help you better understand its spiritual energy, and the reasons for its magical properties.

Many books have been written on the history of herbs, and mythological stories are plentiful; here, however, is a brief overview of herbs and their histories.

Of Herbals and Herbalists

There is evidence that many ancient cultures worked with herbs, from the shamans of Iraq to the ancient Egyptians, Romans, and Greeks. The oldest known herbal is a partial document, the Pen Ts'ao, written around 3000 BCE by Chinese Emperor Shen Nung. It is thought that this document is a compilation of older herbal knowledge that only existed in oral tradition, and that the emperor personally tasted and tested all the herbs listed.

Yet herbs were in use much earlier than this, by prehistoric shamans in a time before humans had fully evolved. Evidence for the use of herbs in healing was discovered in Shanidar, a Neanderthal burial place situated in northern Iraq, thought to be around 50,000 years old. A shaman's grave was uncovered, which included grapes, thistle, hyacinths, cornflowers, and yarrow. It is thought that these herbs and foods were used by the shaman for healing, and that what he had left when he died was buried with him so he could continue to practice in the afterlife.

Ancient herbal wisdom

The ancient Egyptians, with their rich religious history, also used herbs in their rituals. Many herbs were used so often and thought to be so potent that they were sacred in their own right, and whole papyrus scrolls were devoted to the passing on of herbalism for medicine and religious practices. Papyrus was rare and expensive, so this shows how important herbalism was to the Egyptians. The most complete herbal medical papyrus is the Ebers Papyrus, thought to date from around 1550 BCE where herbs such as thyme, juniper, cumin, henbane, bay, caraway, cilantro, elderberry, fennel, garlic, peppermint, and poppy were listed along with their uses. We use the same herbs now—check out Chapter 4 (page 48) for more modern ways of using them in magic and medicine.

The ancient Greeks left extensive medical documents as evidence for their use of herbs. Many plants and herbs were used as far back as 460 BCE, when the "father of medicine" and astrologer, Hippocrates, categorized them into groups for treating various diseases, as well as using herbs and working with the moon phases to treat illnesses successfully. It is said that his favorite herb was parsley, which he used to treat kidney stones and arthritic and rheumatic pain. Soon after him, the first famous botanist and metaphysicist Theophrastus (370–287 BCE) wrote two important books on herbalism, *Enquiry into Plants* and *On the Causes of Plants*, which includes lists of plants usable in medicine, tips on growing them, and precautions. These books had a great influence on medicine right until the Middle Ages.

The Greek physician, Dioscorides, a doctor in Nero's army, wrote extensively on plants and

Take a trip down a historical herbalism path and read "Enquiry Into Plants" by Theophrastus, which is available in an easy-to-read English translation.

Chat with others, especially keen gardeners and elderly relatives and neighbors, about herbs. Many might know of alternative medicinal uses for herbs you didn't know about, or know local mythology of popular local plants!

their medicinal uses—not just in terms of diseases, but also for treating injuries. This knowledge was gained during Nero's bloody campaigns, during which Dioscorides traveled extensively, gaining a herbal knowledge far more wide-ranging than that of herbalists before him. Unlike other Greek doctors and writers, he looked beyond Greece and recorded the use of herbs in other places, giving insight into how herbs were used in many cultures, particularly those that did not write down their herbal wisdom.

Dioscorides is very well known for his Codex Vindobonensis from 512 CE. Made to order for a Roman princess, it has beautiful illustrations of many flowers and plants. Over the years it passed through many hands and kept being annotated with different uses and the names of the listed herbs in different languages. It was bought in 1569 by Emperor Maximilian II for the Imperial library in Vienna, now the Austrian National Library (Österreichische Nationalbibliothek), and has remained there ever since.

Roman herbalism is less well documented, as many of the Roman's physicians were Greek. It is known, however, that the Romans baked anise seeds into bread and wedding cakes, as anise was known for its purification and anti-negativity properties even then. Also, Roman soldiers often carried cilantro (coriander) to help preserve their foods when on long journeys. The Romans were the first to use essential oils extensively, and while there is

some evidence that aromatherapy was used as early as ancient Egypt, the Romans were the first to import oils from all over the world, sometimes establishing trade routes specifically for that purpose.

Despite this, the term "aromatherapy" was not coined until the last century, when Rene Maurice Gattefosse, a French chemist, published his thoughts on the spiritual and healing powers of essential aromatic oils in 1937.

From Ibn Sina to Culpeper

When Europe plunged into the Dark Ages, herbalism went underground and was mostly practiced by "wise women" living in hamlets out of the way of the main towns, as many practices became forbidden once the witch hunts started.

However, not everyone denied the knowledge of the ancients: Islamic culture became a hub of medicinal wisdom, as many Muslim physicians gathered knowledge that threatened to disappear from Europe and Asia, writing it down for future generations. A prime example is Ibn Sina (980–1037 CE), an academic from Persia, who in his work *The Canon of Medicine* (al-Qanun fi at-tibb) blended ancient Persian folk traditions of using herbs in medicine and ritual with the writings of Dioscorides and Galen.

This book was the main herbal bible until 1653, when Englishman Nicholas

Culpeper's *The Complete Herbal* was published. It is likely that Culpeper was the first academic to write a book on herbalism that made the medicinal use of plants and their planetary influences more accessible to the common man. Many witches today still use Culpeper's list of planetary associations. He was also the first to acknowledge the use of herbs by women in *A Directory for Midwives* (1651).

The story of Gilgamesh

In Babylonian mythology, the demigod King Gilgamesh is bitter because he is not immortal; hoping to wring the greatest pleasure from his comparatively short life, he becomes a tyrant, which is easy as he has superhuman strength.

The other deities and his human subjects scheme to cure him of his tyranny. The goddess Shamhat creates a wild man to fight him, Enkidu, who is almost Gilgamesh's equal in excellence, but Enkidu loses the wrestling match and becomes Gilgamesh's friend. In revenge the deities kill Enkidu, since he is human-animal, rather than Gilgamesh, who is god-human.

Gilgamesh, having lost Enkidu, now wants to learn the secret of eternal life. He meets Utnapishtim (a figure similar to Noah from the Old Testament), who has survived a flood, along with his wife, and who are both made immortal by the gods. Utnapishtim's wife tells him of a herb that conveys rejuvenation, if not eternal life. The plant grows on the sea floor (it is thought to be similar to algae, which is very nutritious). Gilgamesh goes out to harvest it, but a serpent steals it from him. So on his way back, Gilgamesh philosophizes to the boatman: the proper ambition of a man should be the building of cities, not the achievement of eternal life. To make amends, he starts worshipping the goddess Ninlil, Goddess of Air, Fields, and Herbs, and builds the city wall for Nippur (the modern Nuffar in Iraq), a city sacred to Ninlil.

Tales of the Irish healer and warrior-god

Dian Cécht is the old Irish God of Healing who healed all the Tuatha De Danann (the heroes and demi-deities of Ireland) after battles. But the Tuatha De Danann were involved in so many fights that it became too much for him, and he decided to bless a sacred well near Slane (northeast Ireland) so the fighters could bathe there and be instantly healed to resume fighting. The water there was so potent in its healing ability that it could cure any illness or injury other than decapitation. It is said that this is where the herb feverfew originally grew. The exact spot of the well has been lost, but there are still several wells around the area, many of which have become Catholic holy wells and are much revered by the local people, Wiccans and Christians alike.

Find local holy wells in your area. In some countries such as Ireland, you can even buy maps where such shrines and other sacred places such as faery forts are listed. If you have difficulty growing a herb you want for your magic, take some of the water from the well and water your seeds or plants with that.

Dian Cécht is also said to be the reason why much of the herbal knowledge of the ancient Irish people and deities got lost. This started with him making a silver arm for his king, Nuada, when the king was injured in battle. Dian Cecht's son Miach, who was taught the healing arts by his father, improved on this by replacing the silver arm with a real one. But that made Dian Cécht jealous of his son's skill, and the father killed the son in envy. This made his other children very sad, especially Miach's sister, Airmed. She cried at Miach's grave for many days and nights, and her tears changed the grass that grew on the grave into over 400 different healing herbs. Again, Dian Cécht was jealous and killed his daughter, too; some stories say as her body fell on her brother's grave, all the herbs died. Other versions say the father pulled from the ground all the herbs other than Irish moss and feverfew, and scattered them into the winds, which is why healing herbs now grow all over the world—although the fact that these herbs have healing properties is often not known.

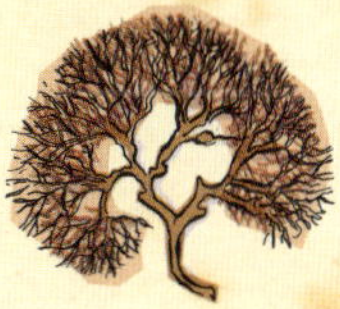

Another Irish story tells of the great warrior, Oisin, who went adventuring in Tir Na Nog when he came across a fair maiden chained to a rock. He tried to free her, but could not. Then the Formorian (a type of evil giant) who had kidnapped the maiden came back from hunting, and injured Oisin badly. As he lay dying, the giant lost interest and fell asleep, as it was late at night. The fair maiden tended to Oisin all night and treated him with healing herbs while saying magical chants over him. As she did so, one of the chains keeping her captive broke. The next morning, Oisin awoke, healed. He fought the Formorian again, without his armor, and this time the fight was more even. In the evening, the giant once again went away to sleep, the maiden tended to Oisin with her magical herbs, and again one of her chains broke. Oisin and the giant fought for seven days, until Oisin buried his sword in the back of the giant's neck and killed him. The last of the chains fell from the fair maiden's waist, and our hero carried her away to safety.

Odin and the Oaths of the Herbs

Baldur, son of Odin and God of the Summer, was afraid he would be killed and had divinatory dreams seeing his death at the hands of the other deities, as they saw it as a challenge to kill him due to his reputed immortality. His mother, the goddess Frigg, took oaths from all herbs, animals, elements, poisons, and diseases not to harm Baldur. She did not ask this oath of mistletoe, because she thought mistletoe was a new plant and therefore too immature to kill or swear not to kill. But the trickster-god, Loki, persuaded Frigg to tell him the details of the oaths of the herbs, and discovered that the mistletoe had not sworn. Loki deceived Bladur's blind brother Hother, God of Winter, into throwing a spear of mistletoe at Baldur. The mistletoe pierced Baldur, and he died instantly. All the deities, even those who tried to kill Baldur themselves, were deeply saddened and decided to burn Baldur's body on a pyre on his ship, which is the traditional Norse burial for heroes. They used mistletoe for kindling as they wanted to destroy the plant. During the funeral, Frigg cried many tears, and her tear drops extinguished the fire and restored Baldur to life. The tear drops remained on the mistletoe as its white berries. In her joy at

having her son back, Frigg kissed everyone who passed nearby, giving rise to the tradition of kissing under the mistletoe.

The Greek myths

Greek mythology is full of herb stories. One tells of Kheiron, a studious centaur who lived on Magnesian Mount Pelion and was the first to discover the use of medicinal herbs—he taught many his knowledge of herbalism, including the famous Asklepios. The renowned witch, Medea, was also a skilled herbalist with extensive knowledge of magical and medicinal herbs. Among other magical feats, she made a cumin and basil ointment for the hero Jason when he prepared to fight King Aeetes' fire-breathing bulls and put the serpent-guardian of the Golden Fleece to sleep with a potion containing wormwood. Medea reputedly left her basket of magical herbs on Mount Pelion, where they sprouted for the use of later Thessalian witches.

Then there is the death of Opheltes, infant son of Lykourgos and Eurydike. The father asked the oracle at Delphi to find out how he might insure the health and happiness of his child. The oracle replied that the child must not touch the ground until he had learned to walk. When the Seven Heroes passed through the town on their way to attack Thebes and asked the slave woman looking after Opheltes for a drink, the slave put the infant down on some wild parsley, where he was killed by a snake. The Seven Heroes renamed the baby Archemoros and held the first Nemean Games in his honor as a funerary festival, giving out crowns made from parsley to the winners.

In another Greek myth, the titan Prometheus made the original humans out of clay, then stole the sacred fire from the gods to give to humans because the people were hungry and cold. In order not to be discovered, he hid the flame in a stalk of fennel. As punishment for the crime, Zeus had him chained to a mountain and sent an eagle to peck out his liver.

Bay is also common in Greek and Roman mythology. Apollo, god of poetry and music, was making fun of love-god Cupid for his small stature and small arrows. So Cupid made Apollo fall in love with a water nymph, Daphne, but made the nymph hate Apollo. The god kept chasing Daphne, who in fear sought the protection of her father, the river god Peneus. Her father was old and knew he wasn't strong enough to fight Apollo, so instead he turned his daughter into a bay tree. Apollo was very sad and cried for the beauty that was Daphne, promising her tree should be forever green, so he would forever remember the nymph's beauty and tend to the tree to make up for his relentless

Part of the Ayurveda, the Atharva Veda, details magical and healing herbs within its mythological stories: the Ashwini brothers, who were human, were given herbal knowledge by Daksha, a powerful god whose responsibility was to fill the earth with living beings. The brothers then passed their knowledge of herbal healing and using herbs in spiritual practice to the weather god, Indra.

Wicca is open-minded, and can take wisdom from all religions. Many of my herbalist friends are Christians who practice witchcraft ("the craft", not the religion of Wicca) and believe the magical energy of herbs comes from their God. These Bible passages tell of the importance of healing plants: Genesis 1:14, 29; Ezekiel 47:12, Psalm 104:14, Ecclesiastes 3:1-8, and Revelations 22:2.

pursuit. To this day, bay leaves are used in wreaths as a sign of victory and honor to poets and conquerors.

Judaism and Christianity

The Judeo-Christian God is definitely in favor of herbs! In Kings 21:2, the need to set land aside to grow herbs is described, and they appear throughout the Old and New Testaments. Wormwood is mentioned as growing in the tracks that the snake made when it was expelled from the Garden of Eden, and God says he will feed the same herb as poison to prideful and false prophets later in the book of Jeremiah. Back in Genesis, Rachel wants mandrakes—known to be love potions even then—from Leah to help her conceive. In the Old Testment, we also find the famous reference to the "bitter herbs" honored on the Seder Plate at Passover (Exodus 12:8 and Numbers 9:11); but what exactly were they? Researchers believe that the herbs referred to were likely a mixture of mint, dandelions, horseradish, and romain lettuce.

Herbs aren't just of importance in the first books of The Bible: Jesus was honoured at his birth with herbs frankincense and myrrh, and later on in the New Testament herbs are mentioned often. In Matthew and Luke, Jesus admonishes the Pharisees for only giving money and not living a godly life by saying they shouldn't just pay their taxes in rue, mint, dill, and cumin, but also use those plants wisely and practice mercy and faith. It is thought the mention of rue in this passage explains why it is still now a symbol of sorrow and repentance (and in witchy terms, used to repent or deflect curses). It may have been nick- named the "herb of grace" in Christian times for the grace given by God following repentance for sins.

Rosemary has its own story to tell. The plant's flowers were said to be white, but became blue as a sign of its repentance when the Virgin Mary snagged her cloak on a rosemary bush while fleeing Herod's soldiers. After this, Christian mythology held that the rosemary plant would never grow higher than 6 feet (just under 2 meters) in 33 years, so that it would never stand taller than the adult Jesus. Rosemary has also become a symbol of fidelity and remembrance, and is often used in wedding celebrations and funerals.

Jesus also used herbs as a metaphor for growth, when he says that a mustard seed is small and insignificant but when grown becomes a large and strong plant, so big that the earth and the heavens meet and the birds rest on it. At the end of his life, when Jesus wore the crown of thorns, it is thought that the crown was made from buckthorn.

Spell brushes made from rue were once used to sprinkle holy water at the ceremony preceding High Mass to cleanse the church spiritually. You can do the same before performing a spell or ritual; use rose water or diluted geranium essential oil for your holy water.

Chapter 3

Growing and Storing Magical Herbs

The best way to get herbs for your magical spells and rituals is to plant and grow them yourself. That way, you know where they have come from, the nutrients they have been given, and what they feel like to live with.

In other words, you know they won't have absorbed the bad energy associated with exploited workers, or have a huge carbon footprint, having been flown thousands of miles from distant countries. You can avoid the use of chemicals on your herbs—which is important, as you may need to eat them as part of a ritual—and you can add your own energies as you tend them while they grow. After all, magic is all about getting the energies right and influencing the universe in a positive way!

The Importance of the Moon Phases when Planting and Harvesting Herbs

The moon is central in magic, and thus also in the growing of magical herbs. Sure, if you have green thumbs, your herbs will probably grow during any lunar phase, but if you plant and harvest your herbs during the correct lunar phase, you are likely to have more success and healthier, bigger plants—and that means more potent magic!

For us witches, the spiritual aspect of the moon is paramount, but there is also a physical reason why you should pay attention to the moon phases when planting and harvesting—the gravity of the moon affects not only the tides, but also the water levels in soil. During a waning moon and especially just before the new moon, the earth's water level is at its lowest, so planting and harvesting herbs at these times makes sense in that you avoid having to work with waterlogged soil.

New moon

The new moon tends to be a bad time for planting or harvesting herbs; it's considered a time of "nothingness" when Mother Earth rests, and so should we (think of it as the witchy Sunday!). The only thing that I would recommend doing now is to remove any dead leaves from plants or do some weeding, although some witches also like to plant and tend evergreen herbs at this time, as they are a sign of hope that the moon will rise again. Instead of working physically with your plants, work mentally at new-moon time: plan what herbs you want to grow next, or design your new herb garden on paper.

Waxing moon

The waxing moon is good for planting most herbs; as the moon grows in the sky, so will your herbs. The exception to this is herbs associated with underworld deities or herbs that have their main active ingredient underground (see waning moon). If you want to go into even more detail, the best zodiac signs of the waxing moon for planting herbs are Scorpio, Taurus, Capricorn, and Cancer. You can look up which zodiac sign rules a particular day online, and there are also whole books dedicated to gardening by the moon (check out the Resources page at the back of this book).

Full moon

The full moon is the best time to harvest plants and herbs above ground because magically, it is the time of completion, of things being perfected. Take note that flowering herbs should generally be harvested during the day, preferably in sunlight if at all possible. If you have to harvest your magical herbs at other times due to your work schedule, because they are getting too big, or it's getting cold outside, consider waiting until the next full moon to "make them magical", i.e., place them on your altar, transfer them into a magical oil, or put them into a charm bag.

Waning moon

The waning moon is a great time to prepare the earth for future planting (filling new plant pots with soil, adding fertilizer to your window boxes, or loosening the sod in your garden,

SPELL

To gain justice, spike an orange with nine cloves and push a sprig of verveine into the top of the orange. Leave it with court/contract papers if you are seeking legal justice, or in a south-facing window if you feel wronged in some other way. Throw away the orange on the next full moon once the situation has been resolved.

ready for planting). Now is also the time to plant herbs that are sacred to the underworld's dark deities such as Hera, who encourages them to grow. These include bulbous plants, potatoes, root vegetables, and root herbs such as ginger—those from which you will harvest their underground parts.

If you have plants that are ready to seed, you can take their seed pods now, dry and prepare them over the next few days, then plant them after the new moon (or keep them for next year's planting, of course). You can prune fruit trees or woody plants at this time, too, as the waning moon tends to force the sap of plants downward.

This lunar quarter is also best for preparing most herbs for long-term storage, as they are more likely to retain their energies and nutritional goodness at this time.

Full moon rituals

Called Esbats, full moon rituals are the traditional meeting day for covens. The moon's energy is at its strongest when it is full, favoring spells and magical rituals. In days gone by, there was also a more practical consideration—covens used to meet in forest clearings or on top of hills at night, and when there was not electrical light, the full moon helped to guide the way. The light of the full moon also helped the witches of old to see and harvest plants such as mistletoe. Mistletoe is traditionally gathered at night, as it is said to be more potent then, and the white berries are easy to see in the light of the moon. Also, because mistletoe is so magical, anyone seen gathering it would have been immediately suspected as a witch. Since witchcraft was considered a serious crime in the Dark Ages, it was best to harvest mistletoe at night, when other people were not likely to pass by.

You do not have to be part of a coven to celebrate the full moon—it serves as a reminder for any Wiccan to practice their spirituality and take a monthly break from the mundane world.

Planting according to the days of the week

You can plant your herbs according to the special influences of each day of the week—for example, you could plant a herb dedicated to the Sun God on a Sunday, and a herb that is used mostly for love magic on Friday, the day of love goddess, Venus. If you have a delicate herb you want to grow well, consider planting it on Tuesday—sacred to Mars—which will give the plant some extra strength. If there is a plant you need to harvest quickly, give it extra attention on Wednesday, the day ruled by Mercury—the planet's influence will help the herb grow quickly and be ready for harvesting soon.

Growing Herbs Indoors

You don't need much space to grow your own magical herbs. Many herbs can be used not only for magical spells and rituals but also for food, magical and otherwise. The kitchen is the idea place for them, especially if you have a window there, but even a countertop will do (and in fact, the best place to germinate seeds tends to be the top of your fridge, as it is nice and warm and out of the way). However, if there is no natural light, you may be limited in the number and type of herbs you can grow—so concentrate on easy-to-grow herbs such as basil, peppermint, and rosemary, which will grow for a time even without any sunlight, and can often be bought in small pots in stores, so if one plant dies, it is easy to replace it.

Herbs by your kitchen window

If you do have a kitchen window, so much the better! The variety of herbs you can grow multiplies, although you will still need to be mindful of the conditions there, such as the quick temperature change when a cold wind comes through the open window, heat from frying up your breakfast, and steam from boiling water and washing up. I also suggest that you keep in mind that herbal magic is all about the energy of not only the herbs but also their environment, so do take this into account when choosing the herbs you wish to grow by your kitchen window.

- First, find out which way your kitchen window is facing—if it is west, you might consider growing herbs associated with water (the element of the west); if south-facing, think about fiery herbs, or those sacred to the Sun God (see Chapter 4 for more details on herbs and their associations with deities and elements).

- Next, keep in mind where the herbs are growing: your kitchen, a place of food. Grow herbs that can do double duty as spices for your food, so giving you a hint of gentle magic every day, even when you do not have time to work an elaborate spell.

- Once you have chosen which herbs you wish to grow, take a moment to think about how you will place them: for example, if you have a little corner shelf with three tiers, and you place the basil (for money) on the top shelf, the chili (for a passionate, fiery relationship) on the middle shelf, and the camomile (for peacefulness) on the bottom shelf, you are effectively symbolizing that money is top of your agenda, and a vigorous (possibly sexual) relationship is more important than having peace in your life. This may be exactly what you want, and if so, fine, but if you long for less stress, you may want to rearrange your herbal shelf!

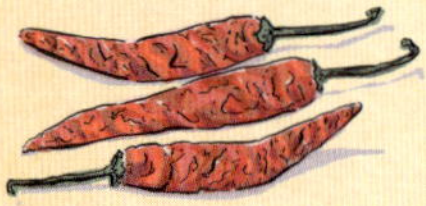

Keep a food diary for a couple of weeks, and look back on the foods you have eaten and find ways in which you can eat healthier. A major way to do this is to replace salt with herbs—get a herbal salt from the health food store or, even better, use some of the magical herbs you're growing! (See the recipe for herbal salt on page 128). You can also use your food diary to find ways to add magical herbs to your daily diet: do you like a bagel with cream cheese for lunch at work? Add some basil to it to help you make money while working! Realize that you feel sluggish after heavy dinners? Drink a cup of fennel or peppermint tea! As well as aiding digestion, fennel boosts energy while peppermint eases any tensions that may have developed during the meal among those eating.

Add some extra energy to your potted herbs by painting the pots a magical color, such as pure and peaceful white for the negativity-busting rosemary, or passionate red for the marjoram you'll add to dishes for your partner. Alternatively, use a departed loved one's favorite mug to grow the verveine you'll use in a meditation to contact them, or an egg cup (the egg symbolizes fertility and growth) to plant herbs such as parsley for fertility or basil for prosperity magic.

SPELL

When you take a sprig from one of your magical kitchen herbs, be sure to say thanks to the plant, and Mother Earth, for providing you with this magical nourishment. It doesn't have to be a long thanksgiving prayer, something as quick as "Lord and Lady I thank thee/For this wonderful herb you've given me!"

Herbs in other parts of the home

The kitchen is the natural place for a witch to grow and use her herbs, but it is certainly not the only place where herbs can grow indoors. If you are careful with your selection of herbs, almost any place in the home, even dark places, can be used to grow magical plants (if nothing else, consider mushrooms for that dark, moldy corner in your basement!).

In the beginning, most herbs need warmth and sunlight to germinate. Once they have four leaves (one for each direction—north, south, east, and west) they are ready to be transplanted into their permanent pot and place to grow. As mentioned above, do be mindful of the energy of the environment in which you are growing your herbs. Herbs to do with love, sexuality, and fertility will do great in the bedroom, and a money plant like basil placed by the front door (to invite in money), or by the computer where you work out your budget, will bring money into the house. You may not want to place them beside your toilet, as the symbolism of flushing away love or money will do nothing for the herb's magical energy!

Do consider the pot you are planting your herbs in; bigger pots make for easier growing and more herbs to harvest, but you may not have the space. If you are lacking space but would like to grow more than one herb, consider a strawberry pot; these are earthenware or clay pots shaped like urns with several side pockets, which allow you to grow a mixture of herbs close together. This works especially well for herbs that complement each other magically, or have similar energies. For example, consider having herbs to strengthen intuition and the self-confidence to follow your intuition, such as tarragon, marjoram, fennel, and basil together. Or, make a "love pot" by planting lemon balm, lavender, catnip, and red clover in a strawberry pot, and crowning it with a mini rose bush. You can also move your strawberry pot to the terrace or garden in summer, and bring it back inside in winter.

CHOOSING POTS

Always choose terra-cotta if you can, as it is about as natural as you can get for a plant pot. It is best to avoid plastic for two reasons: firstly, it is an artificial material and thus doesn't add anything to your magical herb—it could even put some chemicals into the soil—and, secondly, plastic plant pots are usually black, a color symbolizing negativity and generally only used in anti-cursing/negativity spells. If you choose terra-cotta or ceramic pots, you could then think about decorating them too. Paint them in a color associated with the herb you are growing in it (red for love, blue for healing, gold for prosperity, for example) or paint a rune or magical sigil (symbol) representing you and/or the herb you wish to grow, such as an arrow pointing upward for justice.

Both as a witch and a responsible citizen of this earth, I am all for recycling. But be careful when you recycle plant pots! Wash them with soapy water or a vinegar solution first to kill off any fungus or plant disease that may be left over from the last plant.

Growing Herbs Outside your Home

Having a large garden, yard, or other outdoor space for containers in which to grow your own herbs is the ideal way to get magical plants for your spells and rituals, as it means you know exactly where the herbs come from, that they are environmentally friendly, and that you can infuse them with your own energy.

Mother Nature provides for us, and sometimes we don't even realize it. So before you prepare an area of your garden for your magical herbs by weeding it out, take a closer look at what you think are weeds—many of them, such as nettle, have their own magical uses (see page 64).

For growing seedlings until they are ready for planting in bigger pots or in the garden, why not recycle egg cartons? They work great for tiny baby plants that you need to tend individually, and if they are not colored, you can just plant them into the larger pot and they will disintegrate into the soil, thus giving back to Mother Nature.

Growing herbs in the garden

Growing herbs in a garden allows you to grow more herbs, and a larger variety of them; many herbs will not thrive indoors or even in large pots on a terrace, so if you have the opportunity, try these again in your garden and they may grow much better. Some herbs simply need a larger plot of land, or that shady and moist spot under a tree that cannot be replicated indoors. So don't just have one herb plot in your garden, but keep several to allow for different types of herb. If one doesn't seem to work out in one spot, try it in another—even if the growing instructions on the seed packet say it must be planted in shade, maybe your own plant will simply decide that it wants more sun! Be careful when planting some herbs directly into your garden, however—sage, catnip, and verveine grow extremely well, but can easily take over your herb and flower bed in a year or two, so often they are better kept in pots.

When you grow herbs in a garden, you can practice something called "companion planting." This is where you use the energies and physical properties of one plant to help with the growing of another. For example, to help grow cabbage, grow some magical thyme, wormwood, sage, or rosemary nearby. If you grow basil with tomatoes, this will keep pets off the tomato plants, but also the sweetness and nightshade properties of the tomato will balance the strength and sweetness of the basil. However, you should not plant basil close to rue, as rue is bitter and basil is sweet, and thus the two energies jar and neither plant will grow well.

Growing herbs in a window box or terrace

Growing herbs in pots on your windowsill or on a terrace is similar to growing them in a very sunny spot inside, so be sure to read the part of this chapter about growing herbs inside your home (see pages 33-36). There are a few extra things to keep in mind, of course: large pots or window boxes often have bad drainage, which can leave your magical herbs' roots standing in the water and make them rot. You can prevent this by adding a bottom layer of sand to your window box or a few pebbles at the bottom of your plant pot, but why not make this simple task magical by adding some gemstones? Consider tiger's eye for prosperity herbs, clear quartz to strengthen the energy of any herb, or amethyst, to boost any herb's magical potency.

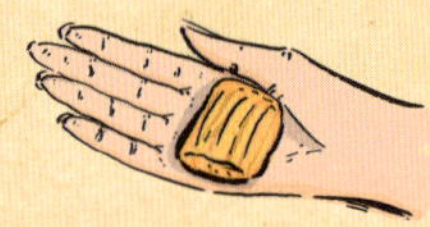

If you find yourself drawn to a particular herb, try out its varieties—the basil family, for example, has a huge variety of subtly different tastes from cinnamon basil to citronella basil. Their different energies can be used in magic, too! Just be careful to plant them a few yards apart so they don't intermingle.

Gathering Herbs in the Wild

Some herbs are difficult to grow even in a large garden, or you may not have access to a garden, but do have time to go walking in the woods on evenings or hiking in the mountains at weekends. Gathering herbs in the wild is a wonderful way to get closer to nature and your local plants, no matter how big your own living space is, or your possible lack of green thumbs. But it is not to be recommended for absolute beginners—so make sure you do your research first with a good field guide to local herbs that includes full descriptions and photographs. Another option is to visit your local botanical gardens or arboretum and ask if the university botany department or park wardens give talks, which will help you get to know and identify local medicinal and magical plants. This is important if you are to collect the right herb rather than misidentify a similar plant, which would be useless for your magical work or even worse, poisonous!

Be careful where you pick your magical plants; don't stray into a fenced-off field or garden, as you don't want to trespass. Consider the energy of a place and its physical location—that catnip may be the only one in the area you can find, but if it's growing in a graveyard, its fun, lighthearted energy will likely be overshadowed by the grief so many people experience there. That wild garlic plant may look healthy, but if it grows near a dump or major road, the toxins from the area will be taken in by the plant and will make it not only bad for eating, but also bad for magic.

Finally, don't be greedy. Only take as much of a herb as you need for your magic, and be sure to put the needs of Mother Nature before your desire to work spells; if a plant is young or if it is small, you may need to leave it alone, even if it is the only one around. And even if that hazel bush seems to have plenty of nuts, please let them be if you know the coming winter is going to be a hard one: birds' and squirrels' need for food to stop them starving comes before your want to do rituals!

Keep a notebook for your wild-herb gathering activities, or leave an area in your Book of Shadows for this. Enter the location of any magical herbs you find; even if the plant is too small this year, you can then return next year and may be able to harvest the magical herb then. Also, take note of any local wildlife and the size of the plants and how much you harvest, so you can monitor the impact of your wild-plant gathering.

If you Cannot Grow your own Herbs or Find them in Nature

While I would always champion the use of homegrown herbs in magic, sometimes this is not possible due to a herb not growing in the climate where the witch lives, or the witch not having the space, tools, or time to grow the herb. In such cases, it is perfectly acceptable to buy a herb. If at all possible, buy a living potted plant (see "herbs by your kitchen window," page 33), and keep it with you for a while before you work with it magically—a few weeks or even a few days will make a difference and allow the plant to attune to your home and personality, and for you to feed it not just water but also your energy, making it yours. Many garden centers, health food stores, and even supermarkets offer fresh potted herbs these days.

If even that is not possible, look for a good supplier for your magical herbs. If your only issue is space—for example, if you live in the middle of a large city—then there may be a friend or relative who can grow some herbs for you, or who is already growing them without knowing they have magical properties, as many magical herbs are also used in simple foods or grown just because they look pretty.

Find out who is a keen gardener among your family and friends and if they might be able to supply you with magical herbs.

I lived in a one-bedroom apartment for several years where I could only grow a few very simple herbs indoors. But my mother had a big house with a garden and, while she was not interested in witchcraft herself, her keen interest in alternative medicine and healing meant she had a well-stocked herbal garden from which I could readily take what I needed when I went to visit. Sometimes she was even able to supply me with ready-mixed herbal teas and teach me about the medicinal uses of herbs I didn't know about! So do check with anyone you know who has a garden to see if they might be able to give you some of their herbs.

If there is no one you know personally who can supply you with herbs, you will need to do some more research to find a good commercial supplier. There are many online, but where possible I would always recommend that you go with a local supplier, such as a health food store or tea house—or a New Age/Wiccan store, if you have such a place near you. That way you can be reasonably sure the herbs are ethically grown and usually organic, too, plus you can look at them and smell them before you buy, ensuring you don't get any moldy, old and dried-out produce.

Make a newly-bought plant yours by visualizing your energy flowing into the plant every time you water it, and holding the pot in your hands with outstretched arms to symbolize the circle of life.

Harvesting and Preserving Herbs for Later Magical Use

You can grow the most beautiful, magically strong herbs you want, but they won't benefit you if you do not harvest them carefully, and think about how you want to store them. Of course when you have your own herbs it's great to use them fresh, but that won't always be possible; so you need to consider the best way to keep them magically potent (and smelling nice, if you plan to eat them) until you come to use them. There are more ways than drying herbs to keep them ready for magic, and below are the best alternative options.

Harvesting

When the time comes for harvest, treat your magical plants with respect and give them individual attention both in the physical act of harvesting, and spiritually. For example, during the growing season, you shouldn't take more than about ten percent of a herb at any one time, and then give it time to regrow and recuperate (how long that takes will depend on the herb—I suggest at least a week, and preferably a lunar cycle, unless it is a fast-growing kitchen herb, such as mint or basil).

If you have annual plants that you will need to re-seed next spring, it is fine to harvest as much as you want of them at the end of the season, and some may even withstand a mild frost and still be useful for magic. But perennials (those herbs and plants that come back again year after year) must be left with enough foliage to conserve their energy so they can withstand winter snow; so it is best to stop harvesting them a lunar cycle or even two before you expect the first frost, so they can have some time to regain their strength.

If you have a flowering herb such as mint, but you will be using only the leaves, try to do your main harvest before the plant comes into flower, as the flowers will take a lot of the energy and essential oil from the plant. Similarly, if you are harvesting the flower from a plant such as camomile, harvest just as the flowers open; that way you acknowledge the beauty of the flower, but still get all its magical energy.

There are many things to take into consideration when

As you get something from Mother Earth by harvesting your crop of magical herbs, give something back: instead of savoring that last bite from your favorite dish or drink, pour it at the root of the plant you are about to harvest.

harvesting your herbs, from the day of the week and the moon phases (see "The importance of the moon phases when planting and harvesting herbs" earlier in this chapter, pages 30–32) to the time of day, which has magical and physical significance. Early morning is a great time for general harvesting; not only does it give you plenty of time to prepare your herbs for storing or magical use, but the herbs have just been symbolically cleansed by the morning dew. Also, their essential oils are strongest at this time because the oils concentrate at night, to be released throughout the day as the sun warms the plant. This doesn't mean that you cannot harvest plants at any time of day, though—you may want to harvest herbs associated with fairies and elves at twilight, and those associated with the Moon Goddess or underworld deities at night, and let the moonlight guide you.

Drying

The easiest way to preserve herbs long term is to dry them—remember that this doesn't mean to dry out plants till they crumple to dust, though! Drying is meant to preserve the plant by removing most of the moisture, so the plant cannot be attacked by fungus or bacteria. It will be dry to the touch, but should retain a little bit of moisture.

It's best not to leave your cuttings laying on the ground for long as their magical energies will naturally flow back into Mother Earth as the plant dies, and you want to keep them within the plant for your magical use. It might seem logical to have the herbs blessed by the Sun God and leave them out in full sunlight as they dry, but that isn't a good idea, either, as it dries them too quickly and the warmth of the sun tends to destroy the essential oils. It is best to place your herbs in a dark or semi-dark place that's dry and warm, but not hot, such as your attic, kitchen cupboard, an unused room, or even your airing cupboard (drying room) if it doesn't get too hot there.

You can lay out individual stems of herbs if you have the space, but I like to gather them in bunches as they look nicer that way, and as I usually use more than one stem at a time anyway, doing this saves space. If you have flowering plants or plants with seed heads still attached, hanging them upside down lets the energy flow into the flowers and helps preserve

them (rather than have the petals fall off), which makes them look nicer when you place them on your altar later.

Another way of drying herbs is to layer them in fine salt; sprinkle an inch or so of salt into a container, then lay down your magical leafy plant or herb, cover well with salt, lay down some more leaves, and so on. After a lunar cycle, the herbs will be dry and you will also have aromatic salt with a subtle herbal flavor that can be used on your altar to symbolize the element of earth, or for cooking. You can do the same with sugar (do be sure to close the jar tightly, so it doesn't attract insects!). However, while you can use salt to dry almost any herb, I recommend that you only use herbs that go well with sweetness when drying in sugar, such as peppermint, lemon balm, lavender, or rose petals.

Pressing herbs

If you want to make magical pictures with pretty magical herbs, or use them as altar decorations, you can press them—simply take some untreated silk paper or blotting paper, carefully place a couple of stems and leaves between two sheets, then place in a book with a rock or some more heavy books on top of it, and leave for a couple of weeks. It's okay to check on the herbs every now and then, but they will dry better and more evenly if left undisturbed.

When you press magical herbs, consider doing so within the pages of a magical book or your Book of Shadows, if you won't be needing it for a while.

SPELL

As you tie your herbs in bunches for drying, work a little magic with this knot spell. Wrap the string around your plants four times (symbolizing the four elements of earth, fire, air, and water), then tie three knots in it while saying:

"Knotting once to begin the magic/Knotting twice to hold it fast/Knotting thrice to keep it safe/Thanks Mother Earth for the blessing you gave!"

Preserving herbs in oil

Most herbs, both leafy and woody, can be preserved in oil, and then used with the oil in all kinds of magical work—from spells and charm bottles to anointing, magical cooking to oil for massaging worries away. It's best to use a mild carrier oil such as virgin olive oil or canola oil when you might be cooking with the magical oil, or rosehip or almond oil if you intend to use the magical oil for rituals, anointing, or massages. I prefer to keep plants as whole as possible to get all of the energy from them, so generally I simply place sprigs of the relevant herb into a bottle of oil and let it infuse for a while (for at least a lunar cycle, but herbs preserved this way will last for a year or more).

Others prefer to make their magical oils more pungent, and chop up herbs, then use about one cup (150 g) of chopped or torn herb with one cup of oil (250 ml). The advantage of this is that it smells stronger, and you don't need to let it infuse for long; a few hours will do. However, I find that these herbal oils don't tend to last as long as oil from infused sprigs.

Freezing herbs

If you want your herbs to be as fresh as possible but cannot use them right away, the best option is to freeze them. Some witches do not like freezing magical ingredients such as herbs and foods as they feel freezing also "freezes out" the magical energy, and also because freezing is usually used to stop negativity (see the spell below). However, I feel that as long as you do this with respect for the herb, making sure that it is thoroughly defrosted before use in a spell or ritual and doesn't have freezer burn or any damage, it is okay to use frozen herbs in magic.

SPELL

To get a person to leave you alone and get out of your life, write their name in black ink or using a black marker pen on a white piece of paper. Place this paper in a container and fill three quarters of it with water (to allow for expansion when freezing). Ensure that the paper is immersed in the water. Place it at the back of your freezer and allow this person to be "frozen out" of your life. Once the negative person has gone, flush the ice away.

How to recognize herbs that are past their best

Because you are harvesting magical herbs for use in spells and rituals, it is important that they are at their best and their energy has been preserved. Sick plants or those that haven't been stored correctly generally won't do any harm (unless you plan on eating them!), but they won't add to your magic, and in fact may stop it from working. Never use moldy plants—if you are using fresh herbs, look at the plant and note any signs of disease, over-watering, or lack of sap or essential oil in the branch or leaf you are harvesting. Check on dried herbs in storage jars or boxes after two or three days (less if it's been a wet day) to ensure they have remained dry and that there is no condensation. If there is moisture, you should be able to save the herb by drying it some more at this time.

When taking magical herbs out of storage, look at the herb and smell it—has it discolored, gone gray? Does it still smell like it is supposed to? If it has lost its aroma or especially if it smells stale, it is probably past its best. Most herbs shouldn't be kept longer than a year, although the bark and roots can generally be kept for two or even three years.

A good tip is to use sticky labels on all your freezer bags, jars of oil, and boxes of herbs, not just stating the name of the herb but also the date harvested and put into storage. I like to include a few other magical factors, such as the phase of the moon, day of the week, and what other herbs I harvested on the same day; when the herb is used up, I then transfer the sticky label into my magical diary with notes on the spell or ritual the magical herb was used in. Over time, this helps me figure out when to best harvest magical herbs, and I can draw correlations between different herbs and when they go off. For example, I have found that magical herbs of the pepper family, especially cayenne and hot chili as well as white pepper corns, seem to lose their magical properties quite quickly although they still smell fine and can be used in cooking.

Just because a herb is past its best and cannot be used for spells or put on the altar, it doesn't mean that it needs to be thrown away; pretty or still fragrant herbs can be used in pot pourris.

Candied herbs and herb jam

If you would like to experiment with more unusual ways of preserving your magical herbs and you like kitchen witchery, why not make some herb jam or candied herbs? Of course not all herbs lend themselves to this, but you can create some wonderful combinations of magical herbs and fruits in jams.

Try boiling some lavender with your elderberries when making jam for a spread that calms frazzled nerves and protects the eater, or try adding some chili to your strawberry jam to spice things up in the bedroom! The possibilities are almost endless, and you can add many herbs either when making the jam, or just before serving it if you buy commercially made or farmer's market jam.

I've recently started making candied herb balls—these are a little trickier than simply adding herbs to a ready-made jam, but they make wonderful presents for witches and just anyone who has a sweet tooth. They are great for very pungent herbs, as the sugar absorbs some of the strong smell and tempers it. To prepare candied herbs you need to heat the sugar to a very high temperature, so this method of preserving doesn't suit delicate herbs, but for herbs such as rosemary, clove, or peppermint, it is perfect. See the recipe below.

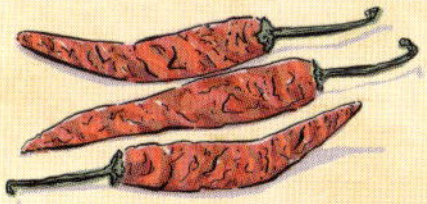

CANDIED HERBS RECIPE

Boil some of your chosen herb in 2 cups (480 ml) water to make a very strong herbal infusion.
Add the infusion and 6 cups (900 g) of sugar in a large saucepan and heat until it bubbles and foams (caution: this mixture is now extremely hot and can easily cause burns).
Pour the mixture into a buttered oven dish and let it cool; when it is warm and mostly set but not hard yet, form into balls or cut into squares.

Chapter 4

The 52 Major Magical Herbs

This chapter is the magical core of this book. It lists 52 magical herbs, arranged by the element they belong to—earth, air, fire, or water. Fifty-two is a rather arbitrary number; I felt that this was enough to cover the main herbs that grow in gardens and in nature (such as basil, peppermint, and wild garlic) as well as those that are easily available from stores (chili, cardamom, and cinnamon, for example) and a few truly magical herbs, like mandrake, that are more difficult to come by, but have an important place in magic.

It is often easier to get hold of an essential oil than a fresh plant, so the non-magical uses of the herbs in this section often make mention of essential oils, which should be diluted in a carrier oil. I have recommended almond or rosehip oil here, but go with whichever oil you prefer—for example, you might like grapefruit oil, jojoba, or olive oil. If you have plenty of the fresh herb, you might consider making your own herbal oil by adding the fresh or dried chopped herb to a little carrier oil. Not only will you have the magical and alternative medicinal properties of the herb, but its texture will also gently exfoliate the skin and get the circulation going.

For each herb, its associated planet, element, and deity are given. Magic is a very individual practice, and so other authors may list other associated planets, elements, and deities for certain herbs; I have listed here what works for me. If the herb you wanted isn't here, check out the Resources section on page 157 for websites and books to help you track down those more obscure herbs.

Earth ☆ North

WILD GARLIC

Planet: Mars

Deity: Hecate, Goddess of the Underworld

Magical uses: Banishing, curse-breaking, inner strength, protection

Non-magical uses: A cut garlic bulb applied to ringworm wounds or other skin infections can help heal them; eating garlic is said to lower cholesterol. It also stimulates the immune system, so is used in the treatment of colds and flu.

SPELL

To stop a person bothering you, write their name with a black pen on a white piece of paper, roll that up and tie a wild garlic plant around it. Bury this as far away from your home as possible.

CUMIN

Planet: Mars

Deities: Prometheus, God of Creation and Strength; Pele, Goddess of Protection and Fire

Magical uses: Physical and spiritual protection, preventing bad luck

Non-magical uses: Prevents flatulence and bloating; can be taken as a tea or, more commonly, simply chewed slowly. A salt and cumin mixture is used to cure a variety of bird diseases, especially in pigeons.

SPELL

Place some cumin seeds under or in an object to prevent theft.

VERVEINE

PLANET: Venus

DEITY: Cerridwen, goddess of shape-shifting; Isis, Goddess of Magic and Children; Kali, Goddess of Death

MAGICAL USES: Peace, psychic protection, healing, magic to help children

NON-MAGICAL USES: The leaves and root can be used in a tea (useful to increase breast milk and to stop diarrhea; it also has a general calming effect) and the flowers for edible decoration. Use crushed fresh leaves in a cool poultice to stop headaches. The Native Americans used to collect the seeds after flowering, roast them, and then grind them into flour used to make little bread-like rolls eaten before rituals.

SPELL

To make an unpleasant person leave you alone, knot together several stalks of verveine and wear them around your neck.

ALLSPICE

PLANET: Mars

DEITY: Aphrodite, Goddess of Love and Compassion

MAGICAL USES: Healing, compassion, luck

NON-MAGICAL USES: Has antiseptic and slight anesthetic properties, is used to help chest infections (usually eaten with food) and ligament and muscle pain (applied to the skin as a rub by adding the herb to some oil, such as almond or rosehip). Allspice encourages digestion and, because of this, is often an ingredient in after-dinner pastries and heavy Germanic winter breads. The berries are lovely in mulled wine and a tea or infusion brewed from the leaves is sometimes used to disguise the bitter taste of other medicinal herbs. The essential oil is used to treat stress and mild depression.

SPELL

To send someone healing, write his or her name on a white piece of paper with a blue pen. Then sprinkle some allspice around the name in a clockwise direction while imagining them healthy and happy. Dispose of the paper when the person is better.

FEVERFEW

PLANET: Venus

DEITIES: Poseidon, God of the Sea and Travel; Aquarius, God of Water

MAGICAL USES: Traveling, physical protection, health, inner strength

NON-MAGICAL USES: When drunk as a tea, can aid relief from migraine headaches; also helps bring on a proper period when you are just spotting. The flowers can cause vomiting. Grows plentifully in hedgerows.

SPELL

To protect yourself when traveling over water, throw a few feverfew flowers overboard as you set off and again when you arrive at port.

TARRAGON

PLANET: Venus

DEITY: Artemis, Goddess of Hunting

MAGICAL USES: Self-confidence, dragon magic (dragon visualizations, in which dragons are guiding spirits)

NON-MAGICAL USES: Tarragon root is used to ease toothache, which can be rubbed directly onto the site of pain. The herb is lovely in scrambled eggs!

SPELL

To increase your self-confidence and drive to achieve a certain goal, eat a dish with tarragon in it just before bed, so the herb may work its magic for you overnight.

PATCHOULI

PLANET: Saturn

DEITIES: Gaia, Goddess of Fertility; Pan, God of Virility and Lust

MAGICAL USES: Virility, sexuality, fertility, divination, money

NON-MAGICAL USES: Used to cover up other smells due to its pungent nature. The essential oil, diluted in a carrier oil such as almond or rosehip and rubbed on the skin can ease dry, chapped skin, acne, and prominent varicose veins.

SPELL

Sprinkle some patchouli in your wallet or rub your wallet with patchouli essential oil; as you do so, imagine the wallet overflowing with money. As long as your wallet smells of this herb, there will always be money in it.

CARDAMOM

PLANET: Mars

DEITIES: Ishtar, Goddess of Love and War; Hathor, Goddess of Music and Beauty

MAGICAL USES: Love, friendship, persuasion, lust

NON-MAGICAL USES: Can be used to flavor coffee, and will lessen the effect of caffeine therein. Helps with PMS (when drunk as a weak tea) and, as a gargle, excess mucus in the mouth (such as after digesting dairy products or when suffering from a mild inflammation of the mouth). In larger amounts, can have a laxative effect.

SPELL

When you need a bit of help persuading someone that you are right (for example, in court or at a business meeting) keep five cardamom seeds in a pocket on your right-hand side.

BLACK PEPPER

PLANET: Mars

DEITY: Zeus, God of Fatherhood and Protection

MAGICAL USES: Protection, inner strength, warding off bad people

NON-MAGICAL USES: Stimulates the taste buds and aids digestion, so great to use when encouraging someone to eat, such as after an illness. Pepper was used as a currency in ancient Rome; when Attila the Hun ransomed the city, one of his demands included 3,000 lbs (around 1360 kg) of pepper.

SPELL

To protect your home or business against thieves, grind some black pepper and sea salt, then mix with vinegar to make a paste. Dab this onto door jambs, window ledges, and any other entrances.

SAGE

PLANET: Jupiter

DEITIES: Chiron, God of Wisdom; Delphi, Oracle of Knowledge

MAGICAL USES: Cleansing, protection, wisdom, animal magic

NON-MAGICAL USES: When drunk as a tea or eaten, helps ease flatulence and bloating. Also helps stop milk when a mother is weaning a baby, but should not be used if you think you may be pregnant other than as incense. Helps calm nervousness and anxiety. Boosts liver function. When applied externally to the skin, diluted sage essential oil (diluted in a carrier oil such as almond or rosehip) or fresh leaves can help heal insect bites, red skin, and soothe inflamed gums (due to teething, wisdom teeth or toothache, for example) until you can get to a dentist.

SPELL

Before a coven meeting or any spiritual work, cleanse the room you will be using by lighting some dried sage and making sure the smoke reaches all the corners of the room.

OREGANO

PLANET: Mars

DEITY: Astarte, Goddess of Health and War

MAGICAL USES: Astral projection, health, happiness

NON-MAGICAL USES: When eaten, oregano can act as a stimulant to treat low energy or mild depression. Drunk as a tea, it can help tension headaches and bring on menstruation. Should never be used in pregnancy, or if you think you may be pregnant.

SPELL

Before astral traveling, rub some oregano on your closed eyelids and say: "I will now sail/To other realms, beyond the veil. Lord and Lady, don't let me fail!"

CARAWAY SEED

PLANET: Mercury

DEITY: Brigit, Goddess of Motherhood

MAGICAL USES: Calmness, de-stressing, meditation

NON-MAGICAL USES: A tea can be drunk to ease stomach discomfort, especially to help heartburn and nausea, or as a gargle to help throat ailments, especially laryngitis. In some Asian countries, gently roasted caraway seeds are served after celebratory meals to aid digestion; it is also said to increase milk production in breastfeeding moms.

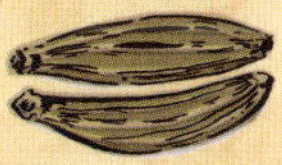

SPELL

To calm yourself before a test or big meeting, chew a caraway seed while saying three times: "Caraway is my balm, I will be calm!"

Air ☆ East

STAR ANISE

PLANET: Jupiter

DEITIES: Apollo, God of Poetry and Music; Hermes, God of Messengers and Travelers

MAGICAL USES: Consecration, purification, curse-breaking, luck, happiness

NON-MAGICAL USES: Used in tonics, and as a tea to ease coughs and colds and to clear the lungs; in ancient Egypt, the seeds were smoked for this purpose. Star anise essential oil (difficult to find) is a great antiseptic. Avoid the oil during pregnancy.

SPELL

To consecrate a new altar or ritual tool, rub some star anise on the object.

LAVENDER

PLANET: Mercury

DEITY: Aradia, Goddess of Witchcraft and Peace

MAGICAL USES: Relaxation, peace, friendship, happiness

NON-MAGICAL USES: Lavender is used to treat unexplained muscle spasms such as eye twitches—you can rub a drop of the oil or the fresh or dried flower around the eye (being careful not to get any in the eye). Or, make a spray with a gentle oil such as almond and dried lavender, and spray over the face (with eyes closed), then massage in gently. Warm lavender baths help circulation, especially if you have cold hands and feet; a few drops of lavender essential oil added to a baby's nighttime bath will help sleep too. A lavender compress can help lower fever. A lavender wash will help most skin issues, from oily skin and acne to insect bites, inflammations, and dermatitis.

SPELL

Friendships will form more easily and heal better after a fight if you wear a lavender-based perfume when meeting the person.

PENNYROYAL

PLANET: Mars

DEITY: Demeter, Goddess of the Harvest

MAGICAL USES: Physical protection, inner strength, money

NON-MAGICAL USES: Taken as a tea to stimulate contractions when labor is slow starting. Not to be used in pregnancy until labor has begun, or if you think you may be pregnant.

SPELL

When walking along a dark road, keep pennyroyal—preferably the flower rather than leaves—near your heart, such as in your breast pocket or in a locket, to help protect yourself.

MARJORAM

PLANET: Uranus

DEITIES: Morrigan, Goddess of Fate and Death; Odin, God of War and Death

MAGICAL USES: Grieving, moving on, inner strength, happiness

NON-MAGICAL USES: Marjoram tea eases bronchial coughs and can also help with tension headaches and anxiety. Drinking the tea and/or massaging some marjoram essential oil (diluted in a carrier oil, such as almond or rosehip) into the lower stomach area can ease menstrual pain. Gently massaging the outer ear and the back of the ear with dilute marjoram oil can help cure ear infections. Marjoram essential oil should not be used during pregnancy, although using small amounts of the herb in cooking is generally considered safe.

SPELL

Use marjoram in dishes at a wake or memorial service to help those left behind grieve and move on peacefully.

EYEBRIGHT

PLANET: Sun

DEITY: Zeus, God of Fatherhood and Protection

MAGICAL USES: Memory, divination, telling the truth

NON-MAGICAL USES: As the name suggests, eyebright is said to help with eye problems—the herb can be rubbed gently on closed eyes—although there is no scientific proof for this. Eyebright tea also helps cleanse the liver after a heavy night of drinking.

SPELL

Keep an eyebright plant where you store your tarot cards, scrying mirror, and similar witchy divination tools. Or, if you cannot find a plant, sprinkle some dried eyebright over the tools. As the name suggests, eyebright helps the eyes, not just physically, but also by opening your "third eye", which sees unseen things, future things, and other planes of existence.

PARSLEY

PLANET: Mercury

DEITY: Persephone, Goddess of Innocence

MAGICAL USES: Contacting the dead, fertility, cleansing, telling the truth. Eating it is said to protect one from speaking wrongly or heatedly

NON-MAGICAL USES: Rich in vitamins A, B, and C as well as trace elements, no wonder parsley is so popular in the kitchen! Taken in food, it can aid circulation and is said to help with kidney and bladder issues due to its blood-cleansing properties. Applied externally, crushed parsley leaves can relieve itching from insect bites or dry skin. While it is fine to eat parsley-flavored foods during pregnancy, you shouldn't eat whole spoonfuls or use the essential oil at this time.

SPELL

Before an important presentation or public-speaking engagement, chew some parsley while thinking about what you are going to say. You will be eloquent and convincing!

BERGAMOT

PLANET: Mercury

DEITIES: Hermes, God of Messengers and Travelers; Fortuna, Goddess of Luck

MAGICAL USES: Luck, curse-breaking

NON-MAGICAL USES: Bergamot is antiseptic; the tea, drunk with a dollop of honey, is used to treat colds, including low fevers and sore throats. It can also relieve flatulence.

SPELL

If you suspect a curse has been placed on you or your family, gargle with cooled bergamot tea or a few drops of bergamot essential oil diluted in a glass of water. Do this at dusk every day from a Full Moon to a New Moon, and the curse will be broken.

PEPPERMINT

PLANET: Venus

DEITY: Aphrodite, Goddess of Love and Compassion

MAGICAL USES: Healing relationships, calming bad situations. Promotes positive emotions; anti-jealousy

NON-MAGICAL USES: Its antispasmodic effects soothe the stomach after a big meal (drinking peppermint tea or eating a peppermint sweet, for example), or when experiencing morning sickness, gas, or colic. It is used, in conjunction with Western medicine, to treat irritable bowel syndrome.

SPELL

If you're having a strained relationship with your in-laws, serve some cooling lemon sorbet with fresh mint leaves on top next time they are over for dinner. Encourage everyone to suck the mint leaves to dispel negative feelings and herald a new, friendlier relationship.

CITRONELLA

PLANET: Neptune

DEITIES: Apollo, God of Poetry and Music; Pax, God of Peace

MAGICAL USES: Happiness, removing obstacles, clear thinking

NON-MAGICAL USES: Commonly used as an insect repellant—by placing the plant near open windows or outside on tables, burning citronella candles, or applying to the skin (cooled citronella tea or citronella essential oil diluted in spring water are common remedies). Can also help relieve excess sweating.

SPELL

To see a person or situation for what it really is, meditate with a citronella plant in front of you.

LEMONGRASS

PLANET: Mercury

DEITY: Cernunos, God of Virility and Health

MAGICAL USES: Lust, psychic powers

NON-MAGICAL USES: Lemongrass tea is drunk after an illness to boost the glandular, immune, and digestive systems. It also gives a general energy boost, relieves nervousness, and helps with jet lag. The crushed grass, or essential oil diluted in a carrier oil such as almond or rosehip, can be applied directly to the skin to relieve muscle spasms such as eye and mouth twitches, or leg cramps after exercise. Applied the same way to skin, it is also used to treat ringworm, other parasites such as lice, and athlete's foot.

SPELL

To spice up your sex life, make a braid with three stalks of lemongrass and place this around a photo of you and your lover.

Fire ☆ South

CHILI

PLANET: Mars

DEITIES: Vulcan, God of Fire; Durga, Goddess of Beauty and Power

MAGICAL USES: Lust and virility, excitement, new ideas, protection from evil spirits

NON-MAGICAL USES: Can ease pain, especially backache; also reduces itching. Usually the seeds are added to a cream or oil and applied to the skin, but chili is also effective when eaten in food.

SPELL

To spice things up in the bedroom, rub a red candle with chili oil from the base to the top, then light it.

CINNAMON

PLANET: Sun

DEITIES: Helios and Ra, Gods of the Sun; Oshun, Goddess of Love and Lust

MAGICAL USES: Love and lust, power, success, knowledge

NON-MAGICAL USES: Cinnamon is an astringent, a stimulant, and an antiseptic; sipping some warm water with a cinnamon stick swirled in it can help stop vomiting. The essential oil is famed for its antibacterial and antifungal properties, but also has other uses; a few drops mixed with some banana mash can help relieve flatulence and diarrhea. There is some evidence that eating a teaspoon of ground cinnamon a day can help with high cholesterol and reduce blood-sugar levels, but more research is needed. While it is fine to eat cinnamon-flavored foods during pregnancy, you shouldn't eat whole spoonfuls or use the essential oil at that time.

SPELL

To attract a new mate, sprinkle some cinnamon on a heart cut out of red paper. Fold the paper three times to contain the cinnamon within, and leave somewhere safe until you have started a new relationship.

DILL

PLANET: Mercury

DEITY: Brigit, Goddess of Motherhood

MAGICAL USES: Lust, overcoming obstacles, seeing the positive, helping children

NON-MAGICAL USES: Dill aids digestion—add some dill seeds to a heavy dish or serve dill leaf tea after a big meal. It is great for relieving colic and the associated stomach upset, even in small children (see the gripe water recipe in Chapter 7). Chew dill seeds to clear your breath after eating garlic, or just to freshen your breath. Dill rubbed on the skin promotes healing.

SPELL

Add dill to a warm bath before meeting your date and taking your relationship to the next level.

MANDRAKE

PLANET: Mercury

DEITIES: Aphrodite, Goddess of Love and Compassion; Circe, Goddess of Divine Beauty

MAGICAL USES: Fertility, strength, protection from magic. Mandrake also strengthens the energy of any magic when placed on the altar during a ritual, or when working a spell

NON-MAGICAL USES: The leaves are cooling and can be used in poultices to reduce fever or ease sunburn. The root and bark are toxic and should not be ingested.

SPELL

Sleep with a whole mandrake root under your pillow when trying to conceive.

RED PEPPERCORN

PLANET: Venus

DEITY: Izanami, Goddess of Creation and Birth

MAGICAL USES: Love and sexuality magic, telling the truth, self-confidence, health

NON-MAGICAL USES: When ingested, will ease constipation and is said to lower fever. Roughly ground and mixed with a carrier oil such as almond or rosehip, it can be rubbed on arms and legs to increase circulation.

SPELL

Wanting to spice up your relationship in the bedroom? Take eight red peppercorns; put two in your lover's food, two in your food, two under his pillow, and two under yours. Then go and have fun!

BAY

PLANET: Jupiter

DEITIES: Apollo, God of Poetry and Music; Ceres, Goddess of Food and Wisdom; Delphi, Oracle of Knowledge

MAGICAL USES: Success, knowing the future, wisdom

NON-MAGICAL USES: Dried leaves and bay oil are used in cooking and have a mild stimulant effect. Bay leaves are antifungal and an extract of bay—3½ oz (100 g) of the herb to around 13½ fl oz (just under half a liter) of alcohol can be used to treat athlete's foot and similar problems. Bay-leaf wreaths are used in Wiccan rituals, and historically they signified a very important person, usually an Emperor.

SPELL

In the kitchen, only the dried leaf is used but in magic, the beautiful reddish-blue berries are also used—if you feel that the previous occupant of your newly purchased home has left negativity or you are unsure about the intention of a house guest, place some bay berries in a small white bowl. The berries will turn black within a few days if negativity is indeed present. If they are still red a week later, no bad feelings are around.

NETTLE

Planet: Mars

Deities: Thor, God of Thunder and Healing; Helios, God of the Sun; Apollo, God of Poetry and Music; Oya, Goddess of Wind and Change

Magical uses: Protection, healing, curse-breaking

Non-magical uses: Nettle leaves are full of iron and potassium, so a nettle tea or salad is great for treating anemia and is safe even in pregnancy (boil the leaves briefly before eating to take out the sting). Drinking nettle tea and eating the leaves is also said to be helpful in the treatment of asthma and to help regulate blood sugar levels (in conjunction with traditional Western medicine, of course); and a nettle infusion rubbed into the scalp will reduce the oiliness of hair. The root, boiled and drunk, can ease common allergies.

SPELL

Sew a large nettle leaf into your clothing, stinging side facing out, to protect yourself from physical harm and to send any curse aimed at you right back.

CLOVE

Planet: Jupiter

Deity: Morrigan, Goddess of Fate and Death

Magical uses: Protection, curse-breaking, removing curses

Non-magical uses: Chewing cloves, or drinking them in tea, can help with digestive issues, especially bloating and cramping. Can also help kill internal parasites, such as worms, and ease allergy and hay fever symptoms as it has mild antihistamine properties. If you have toothache, bite down on a clove to ease the pain until you can get treatment from a dentist.

SPELL

Put a drop of clove essential oil onto the sole of each shoe in the morning to protect yourself from magical and spiritual assaults.

ROSEMARY

PLANET: Sun

DEITIES: Zeus, God of Fatherhood and Protection; Hera, Goddess of Purification and Marriage

MAGICAL USES: Banishes negativity and nightmares, cleansing and purifying, protection, memory spells. Rosemary is often burnt to cleanse an area before casting a magical circle.

NON-MAGICAL USES: A rosemary-and-oil rub is said to help slow down hair loss by boosting the circulation; it also tones the scalp to avoid dandruff (wash your hair, massage in the rosemary and oil, leave for a few minutes, then wash again). Rosemary contains lots of iron and vitamin C, making it a great tea for the cold months of the year. The flowers look great in a salad! While it is fine to eat rosemary-flavored foods during pregnancy, you shouldn't eat whole spoonfuls or use the essential oil at that time.

SPELL

If you have a child who has nightmares or fears the monster in the wardrobe, cast a simple circle of protection around his or her bed by sprinkling some dried rosemary in a clockwise circle, starting at the head of the bed. Let the child do it themselves if they are interested in magic.

JUNIPER

PLANET: Sun

DEITY: Jupiter, God of Psychics

MAGICAL USES: Psychic awareness, protection

NON-MAGICAL USES: Juniper is used to treat minor bladder and kidney problems, as well as indigestion, flatulence, and water retention. Usually, the juniper berries are added to a little oil, such as almond or rosehip, and applied to the skin, which also boosts the circulation. The berries taste lovely in vinegar used for pickling vegetables or fish, or to flavor game and stuffing, or even with coleslaw. Don't eat it or use the oil during pregnancy.

SPELL

Burn juniper berries on a charcoal disk and inhale the smoke before doing a visualization, deep meditation, or trying to see otherworldly entities such as fairies and spirits.

NUTMEG

PLANET: Jupiter

DEITIES: Herne, God of Prosperity and Food; Loki, God of Fire and Tricks

MAGICAL USES: Luck, fortune-telling, money

NON-MAGICAL USES: Nutmeg used in foods will stimulate the appetite, especially after an illness, as it can help prevent nausea; will also help prevent flatulence by moving food along the intestinal tract. Used to treat minor morning sickness, nutmeg essential oil or a strong nutmeg infusion can also ease toothache and skin complaints, such as dermatitis and eczema.

SPELL

Rub your resume with a cut nutmeg before sending them out for extra luck getting a job.

BASIL

PLANET: Mars

DEITIES: Aradia, Goddess of Witchcraft and Peace; Vishnu, God of Money; Loki, God of Fire and Tricks; Ares, God of Determination and War

MAGICAL USES: Money, prosperity, fortune-telling, inner strength

NON-MAGICAL USES: Rubbed on the skin, crushed leaves or basil essential oil (diluted in a carrier oil such as almond or rosehip) can alleviate stress-induced skin issues, such as contact dermatitis. When taken in food, it encourages proper digestion and helps ease stomach cramps. Drinking basil tea when exhausted promotes relaxation and sleep—however, the taste can be a bit strong for most people. Basil should not be used by pregnant women.

SPELL

Fry some basil in batter before asking for a raise or seeing your bank manager about a loan; the combination of gold and green colors and the basil will draw money to you!

MUSTARD

PLANET: Mars

DEITIES: Toth, God of Wisdom; Juno, Goddess of Fidelity and Protection

MAGICAL USES: Protection, purification

NON-MAGICAL USES: Rubbing whole mustard seeds onto the skin can stimulate circulation and relieve muscle pain.

SPELL

Bury five mustard seeds at each corner of your property to protect it from thieves and vandals.

HAWTHORN

PLANET: Mars

DEITY: Lady Godiva, British heroine

MAGICAL USES: Wishes, fertility, lust, protection, fairy magic. Sacred to the Druids; used to decorate the maypole and to make magic wands

NON-MAGICAL USES: Hawthorn berry tea is drunk to improve circulation, especially in the hands and feet, and to lower blood pressure. The tea or syrup is also used in the treatment of insomnia and as a memory aid for older people or those who are stressed. In the nineteenth and early twentieth centuries in times of need, such as during war, young hawthorn leaves were used as substitutes for tea and tobacco, and the seeds were ground in place of coffee.

SPELL

To have a wish granted, get a piece of cloth of an appropriate color (green for prosperity, red for lust, black for protection, for example). At night, go to a hawthorn bush, hold the cloth while thinking of your wish, spit into the cloth, then tie the cloth onto the tree.

JASMINE

PLANET: Moon

DEITY: Venus, Goddess of Love

MAGICAL USES: Romantic love, meditation, dreams, fortune-telling

NON-MAGICAL USES: Dab some cooled jasmine tea on red or burning eyes to ease them. A strong infusion, gargled, can be used to treat mouth ulcers. Jasmine is a great tonic for the skin—use on red or warm skin after sun and wind burn, or bathe in jasmine flowers or with a few drops of jasmine essential oil to treat dry and stressed skin (great for contact dermatitis). Can also be used to treat mild depression.

SPELL

To move a relationship from friendship to something more, sprinkle jasmine flowers onto a photo of the two of you in a heart shape.

BUCKTHORN

PLANET: Jupiter

SPIRIT: Elves, who can help with money magic

MAGICAL USES: Helps with finances, wards off the evil eye

NON-MAGICAL USES: Boiled with honey it eases constipation and acts as a diuretic. Buckthorn tea is used to treat gallstones, in conjunction with Western medicine. Used as a purgative for animals, such as when a dog has eaten chocolate and needs to regurgitate it. Do not use if pregnant or breastfeeding.

SPELL

When business isn't going well or your personal finances suffer, and you suspect it is because someone wishes you ill, burn some buckthorn on the flame of a black candle while saying: "Whatever evils my finances have here I'll cast them back, I have no fear!"

CAMOMILE

PLANET: Mercury

DEITY: Cernunos, God of Virility and Health, sacred also to all Egyptian deities

MAGICAL USES: Health, meditation, calmness, luck

NON-MAGICAL USES: Camomile tea is used as a mild sedative, to cure insomnia, and ease stomach cramps and aches, especially menstrual cramps. A cool tea or mild infusion given in a bottle or cup to teething babies will lessen discomfort. Great as an anti-inflammatory and to ease rheumatic pains, it can be applied as an ointment or by rubbing crushed flowers directly onto the skin. A salve (see the recipe in Chapter 7) applied externally will ease hemorrhoids and sunburn. Camomile tea can also be used as a tonic for other plants.

SPELL

Nervous before a big test or job interview? Sprinkle camomile flowers in a clockwise motion around your bed before you go to sleep for a restful sleep and to increase your luck!

IRISH MOSS

PLANET: Neptune

DEITIES: Cerridwen, Goddess of Shape-shifting; Gwydion, God of the Arts and Gambling

MAGICAL USES: Business success, good luck, gambling

NON-MAGICAL USES: Stimulates appetite and the healing of wounds; soothes a sore throat and irritated membranes. Irish moss has lots of iron, and can be added to a salad, fried and eaten as a side dish, or mixed into mashed potatoes.

SPELL

Sprinkle some Irish Moss under the welcome mat or under the carpet of your business to attract a steady stream of paying customers.

CHIVES

PLANET: Uranus

DEITIES: Lyr, God of the Sea; Saraswati, Goddess of Self-knowledge

MAGICAL USES: Relaxation, seeing things positively, breaking bad habits

NON-MAGICAL USES: May reduce blood pressure, help regulate blood sugar levels, and promote relaxation. Can help newly hatched birds survive by stimulating appetite. Are you trying to stop smoking or cutting down on alcohol? Whenever you feel the need for a cigarette, chew some chives instead.

SPELL

To break a bad habit or see something in a more positive light, place a symbol of the issue (such as a cigarette, if you are trying to stop smoking, or a photo of your in-laws if you are having trouble with them) on a white plate. Take five blades of chive and arrange them in a pentagram shape around the symbol. Leave this undisturbed until the issue has been resolved.

EUCALYPTUS

PLANET: Moon

DEITIES: Ogun, God of Iron and War; Brigit, Goddess of Motherhood

MAGICAL USES: Lucid dreaming, protection, health

NON-MAGICAL USES: Great to help breathing when you have a cold or bronchial issues—boil some leaves and inhale the steam or add a few drops of eucalyptus essential oil to your bath. Make a balm to have on hand for pulled muscles and sprains (see the recipe for ointment in Chapter 7, page 127). Undiluted essential oil, dabbed on abscesses and warts, will help them recede.

SPELL

To aid you in lucid dreaming, sew some eucalyptus leaves into a purple pillow and sleep on it.

HEMLOCK

PLANET: Saturn

DEITY: Hermes, God of Messengers and Travelers

MAGICAL USES: Warding (magical protection against negative energy and spiritual entities), astral projection

NON-MAGICAL USES: Poisonous! Can paralyze, and should not be used by lay people.

SPELL

Some witches keep a dried hemlock branch in their Book of Shadows or with their magical tools to keep their magic secret.

FENNEL

PLANET: Mercury

DEITY: Baal, God of Courage

MAGICAL USES: Motherhood, courage, inner strength

NON-MAGICAL USES: A few drops of fennel essential oil added to warm water as a drink can help with gas and heartburn, and will increase menstruation and urine flow as well as increase breast milk, but should not be used during pregnancy. Fennel syrup can ease a chronic cough. Gargle with cooled fennel tea to treat gingivitis and sore throats.

SPELL

Throw fennel seed instead of rice or confetti at a wedding if the couple wishes to conceive soon.

THISTLE

PLANET: Jupiter

DEITY: Morrigan, Goddess of Fate and Death

MAGICAL USES: Courage, standing up for your beliefs, fairies

NON-MAGICAL USES: Eases sore throats (as a gargle) and can be used to treat jaundice, when the essential oil is diluted with a carrier oil, such as almond or rosehip, and applied to the skin. Can help in cases of mild depression and stress—drink as a tea or inhale a few drops of the essential oil from a tissue or napkin.

SPELL

To get extra courage to solve a problem or to stand up for what you believe in, cup a thistle flower between your palms while imagining yourself in the situation and resolving it successfully.

CATNIP

PLANET: Venus

DEITIES: Bast, Goddess of Cats; Sekhmet, Goddess of Healing and Beauty

MAGICAL USES: Fun, animal magic, beauty

NON-MAGICAL USES: Great for repelling mosquitoes! Some cats act as if "high" on it. The plant can act as a stimulant or sedative for humans, so eat a little and test its effects first! Catnip also stimulates sweating and thus can help break a fever. A weak catnip infusion massaged into the scalp will reduce dandruff, and dabbed on swollen and puffy eyes will ease them. A strong catnip infusion can be used as a flea-repellent bath for animals or as an anti-flea shampoo for carpets.

SPELL

Add some young catnip leaves to a salad for a party to ensure great fun on the night!

VALERIAN

PLANET: Venus

DEITY: Arianrhod, Goddess of Fate

MAGICAL USES: Peaceful relationships, friendship, dream magic (see Chapter 1, page 17)

NON-MAGICAL USES: A great aid for any sleep issues, from general insomnia to stress-induced sleeplessness or noise issues. Strong valerian tea (made with the root) is given after a stressful event to ease the mind and body, and normal strength valerian tea can be drunk to ease PMS and menopausal symptoms.

SPELL

Add some crushed valerian leaves or dried valerian to your bath water before attempting dream magic, such as encouraging lucid dreaming or divinatory dreams.

LEMON BALM

PLANET: Moon

DEITIES: Arianrhod, Goddess of Fate; Selene, Goddess of the Moon and Healing

MAGICAL USES: Healing, love, anti-stress. In medieval times, a lemon balm plant near the front door was said to drive evil spirits away.

NON-MAGICAL USES: Antibacterial and antiviral. Applied to fresh insect bites, it will lessen itching and swelling, and it is used in the treatment of cold sores and the herpes simplex virus—crush a leaf and apply directly, or use a strong cooled lemon balm tea. The tea also makes a refreshing drink to treat depression and anxiety. It's very easy to grow!

SPELL

If you or a friend are sick, place five lemon-balm leaves, arranged in the shape of a pentagram (i.e., with round ends touching) on top of a photograph of the sick person. Leave it where the moonlight can shine on it until they are getting better.

RED CLOVER

PLANET: Mercury

DEITY: Rowan, Goddess of Luck

MAGICAL USES: Luck (especially the four-leaved clover), prosperity, happy relationships

NON-MAGICAL USES: Used to treat breathing and skin problems as well as PMS. Gentle enough to be used on children's skin. The tea can be drunk or, when cooled, applied to the skin, or the essential oil diluted in almond or rosehip oil, then applied.

SPELL

Dry a four-leaved clover and keep it with your test papers when preparing for an exam or driving test to help you succeed.

THYME

PLANET: Venus

DEITIES: Lakshmi, Goddess of Wealth and Purity; Ganesha, God of Success

MAGICAL USES: Concentration, healing, business success

NON-MAGICAL USES: Drinking thyme tea or inhaling the steam from an infusion can ease coughs and tonsillitis. Thyme is antiseptic and antifungal, and gargling can help treat gingivitis and other gum diseases (gargle with strong cooled thyme tea, or with a few drops of the essential oil added to warm water). Make a strong infusion and massage into the scalp to treat a dry, itchy scalp and dandruff. While it is fine to eat thyme-flavored foods during pregnancy, you shouldn't eat whole spoonfuls or use the essential oil at that time.

SPELL

Burn thyme before studying before an exam to improve concentration—either by burning the herb on an open fire or by using the essential oil in an aromatherapy burner.

CAMPHOR

PLANET: Moon

DEITY: Artemis, Goddess of Hunting

MAGICAL USES: Occult knowledge, psychic arts, past lives

NON-MAGICAL USES: Used as an inhalation, it stimulates the nervous system and circulation (thus used to wake people who have fainted)—and helps relieve menstrual pain. A very diluted camphor compress can also help menstrual pain, and treat chapped lips. A couple of drops of camphor to oil/fat make a lip balm (see the recipe for nourishing lip gloss in Chapter 7, page 138). Do not use the oil undiluted on the skin.

SPELL

Wash with camphor soap before working magic and/or put some camphor-based mothballs in your ritual robes when not wearing them to help you retain magical and occult knowledge.

WORMWOOD

PLANET: Mars

DEITY: Rusalki, the Russian snake spirit

MAGICAL USES: Healing, protection from evil spirits

NON-MAGICAL USES: A few drops of wormwood essential oil in warm water can be drunk as a tonic, and to reduce fever. It can also be used to treat worms in humans and animals. The leaves can be made into a tea, which eases pain, and has traditionally been used to treat labor pain. The essential oil, diluted, is applied to soothe insect and snake bites and draw out the poison. Only use in a very diluted form, as pure wormwood can be poisonous. The liquor absinthe is made from wormwood.

SPELL

If you feel that bad spirits work against your spells, place a piece of wormwood or a few drops of wormwood essential oil on your altar or Book of Shadows to ward your magic.

Chapter 5

Other Foods and their Magical Uses

This being a Herbal, herbs, of course, take center stage in the magic, alternative medicine, and other ways to use plants described in this book. Yet the definition of herbs is fluid when it comes to herbalism and the magical use of herbs—several of what we term "herbs" are not in fact herbs in the biological sense (for the curious, the dictionary definition is "A plant whose stem does not produce woody, persistent tissue and generally dies back at the end of each growing season").

Also, oftentimes in magic, especially in kitchen witchery, herbs are not used in isolation but in combination with other plants and foods to make a magical dish (for example, see the Cakes and Ale ritual in Chapter 1, page 19).

Because of this, I have added what sort of herb the food is often combined with and how—these are just examples, so do experiment with your own combinations. There are of course many magical foods (which probably deserve their own book), and in this chapter I have listed a number of foods that are commonly combined with herbs for their magical uses, or are used in ways similar to herbs.

Earth ☆ North

ALFALFA

Planet: Venus

Deity: Vishnu, God of Money

Magical uses: Money, prosperity

Non-magical uses: Used to treat infections, especially cuts, by applying the crushed leaf or an alfalfa salve (you could make this by adding herbs to a light moisturizer). A few drops of the essential oil or crushed leaves can be added to a carrier oil such as almond oil, warmed and applied to the outer ear with a cotton bud to help heal the outer ear after ear infections. A super plant with antioxidants as well as many vitamins, this is a great food plant—so much so that the Arabs used to feed it to their prized horses!

Often combined with: Basil. Eaten in a salad or baked dish, will draw money to you.

SPELL

On a Thursday, sprinkle alfalfa in the coin section of your wallet and in your safe if you have one to draw money to you.

BLACKBERRY

Planet: Saturn

Deity: Brigit, Goddess of Motherhood

Magical uses: Protection, healing

Non-magical uses: Tea made from blackberry root is drunk to treat diarrhea and hemorrhoids, and gargled with to ease sore throats; diluted tea can be used to bathe sore and red eyes. Crushed berries applied to the skin can lessen acne and beautify oily skin, as well as help small open wounds and scratches stop bleeding and close. Young blackberry shoots are eaten as a salad in spring to cure cystitis.

Often combined with: Allspice and sugar. Sprinkled over blackberries, this dish is traditionally given to people in need of healing.

SPELL

Tape a blackberry thorn on each of the four corners of the back of a loved one's photo to protect them.

WHEAT

Planet: Mars

Deities: Juno, Goddess of Fidelity and Protection, and Brigit, Goddess of Motherhood

Magical uses: Fertility, money, prosperity. Brigit's crosses (made especially for May Day) are woven from wheat stalks

Non-magical uses: A great source of protein and carbohydrates

Often combined with: Parsley, which is baked into wheaten bread and eaten before a hoped-for conception.

SPELL

Put some wheat in your cauldron or in a bowl on a new moon and keep it constantly damp. On the full moon, if it has started sprouting, eat it to make your wishes for money or fertility come true.

WALNUT

Planet: Venus

Deity: Durga, Goddess of Beauty and Power

Magical uses: Desirability, mental powers, fertility

Non-magical uses: The outer green skin can be applied directly to the skin to protect wounds, as it contains natural iodine; the skin is also chopped up and eaten to relieve diarrhea and anemia. The nut rubbed on the skin will lessen skin complaints, from eczema and acne to sunburn and chapped lips. To make a natural antiperspirant, boil the leaves of the walnut tree; bathe your feet and hands in the cooled infusion, and dab on the underarm area.

Often combined with: Catnip, and left in the bathroom to boost your beauty (display a small plate of catnip and walnut, or a catnip plant with a few walnuts surrounding it).

SPELL

To make yourself more desirable to the opposite sex, take two walnuts and crush them between your palms while thinking of the ideal traits your future partner will have. Then eat the walnuts and keep the shells under your bed until a new partner shares it!

Air ☆ East

ALMOND

PLANET: Mercury

DEITY: Toth, God of Wisdom

MAGICAL USES: Money, prosperity, wisdom

NON-MAGICAL USES: The nut is eaten to ease constipation. Almond milk can be made from ground almonds diluted with water, and can be used for babies and adults who are allergic to cow's milk. Almond oil is a great carrier oil for essential oils, particularly for medicinal massages; almond oil alone can help heal rough, chapped, dry, or red skin.

OFTEN COMBINED WITH: Pennyroyal, and carried in the wallet to attract money.

SPELL

To always have money, place seven almonds in your pocket each Thursday, and eat one at exactly noon each day.

BLUEBERRY

PLANET: Uranus

DEITY: Tengri, God of the Sky

MAGICAL USES: Protection, the occult arts. Often used to represent the color blue when something edible is needed

NON-MAGICAL USES: Eaten to ward off bladder problems, especially bladder infections, and treat diarrhea. It is said to improve vision when eaten regularly. There is some evidence that it keeps blood pressure and harmful cholesterol low.

OFTEN COMBINED WITH: Mandrake. Mandrake and blueberries can be kept on the altar during complex magic, to help the magic be more powerful.

SPELL

A way of choosing what tarot cards to read is to place them all on a table face down and then throw a number of blueberries across the cards. Read those cards the berries landed on.

HAZELNUT

PLANET: Sun

DEITY: Gwydion, God of the Arts and Gambling

MAGICAL USES: Luck, divination, protection. It is carried in Germanic countries to ward off lightning.

NON-MAGICAL USES: Eaten to strengthen the immune system and get a sluggish digestive system going. Contains lots of potassium and B vitamins.

OFTEN COMBINED WITH: Nutmeg in cookies to attract luck.

SPELL

While sitting comfortably on the floor, take a handful of hazelnuts then think of a question. Let the nuts fall onto the floor, and interpret any shapes they make. How many roll far away can also give you an indication of the magnitude of your problem—for example, if they are scattered widely, then the problem may be bigger; affecting more people, than you had thought.

MISTLETOE

PLANET: Sun

DEITY: Freya, Goddess of Love

MAGICAL USES: Romantic love, protection from evil, conception, dreaming, hunting

NON-MAGICAL USES: Mistletoe is used with a carrier oil, such as almond or rosehip, as a rub to treat the symptoms of arthritis. To treat dizziness, it can be drunk as a tea, or added to alcohol (it could be made in advance and carried with you). This plant is somewhat poisonous, and should not be ingested unless you are familiar with its properties.

OFTEN COMBINED WITH: Buckthorn, to help those troubled in love. Can be used to flavor mead (the honey drink) or in a spell to gain closure on a situation.

SPELL

To protect your loved one while they are traveling or working with bad people, take a branch of mistletoe with as many leaves as days they are away working. Impale a rose petal on each mistletoe leaf, first kissing the petal. Each morning, take a petal off the mistletoe branch and thank Freya or your own patron deity for the protection she has given. You can repeat this spell as needed.

Fire ☆ South

CORN

PLANET: Jupiter

DEITY: Adonis, God of Lust

MAGICAL USES: Virility, lust, friendship

NON-MAGICAL USES: Corn silk (the "hairs" of a sheaf of corn) is boiled and drunk to treat urinary infections and to cure bedwetting in children; it also stimulates the appetite.

OFTEN COMBINED WITH: Catnip—the catnip leaves are wrapped around the corn and kept in a room where you are having a party, or served as a mixed salad, to make the party extra fun.

SPELL

To increase a man's sexual prowess, place a corn stalk (red corn is even better than yellow) under the bed.

GINGER

PLANET: Mars

DEITY: Artemis, Goddess of Hunting

MAGICAL USES: Used in love spells as well as money and general business success spells.

NON-MAGICAL USES: When eaten or drunk as a tea, it will stimulate the senses and prevent gas. Candied ginger is great for preventing and curing morning sickness and sea sickness. Juiced ginger is drunk to help with hangovers and diarrhea.

OFTEN COMBINED WITH: Lavender, in cold drinks to give to your lover. The drink increases romance as well as happiness and peace in your relationship.

SPELL

Chew a piece of ginger before any spell, but especially love or prosperity spells, to increase your power in working the magic.

GOLDENSEAL

PLANET: Sun

DEITY: Aradia, Goddess of Witchcraft and Peace

MAGICAL USES: Healing, inner strength. Goldenseal is sacred to the Native Americans

NON-MAGICAL USES: The crushed leaf applied to a wound or sore will act as a mild antibiotic and help stop bleeding. A tea made from the root is drunk to aid digestion and stimulate the appetite, as well as to treat dehydration. The tea is also drunk to treat pelvic inflammatory disease, together with traditional medicine. Goldenseal should not be taken during pregnancy, and should not be taken long term (a month at the most), as it can kill beneficial bacteria in the gut.

OFTEN COMBINED WITH: Irish Moss and put in witch bottles (see Chapter 1, page 16) for healing.

SPELL

Place a piece of goldenseal in a golden locket and wear it around your neck with a blue piece of cord or ribbon to protect yourself from illness and injury.

LIQUORICE

PLANET: Mercury

DEITY: Hecate, Goddess of the Underworld, Magic, and the Occult

MAGICAL USES: Talking to ancestors, helping ghosts move on, love magic

NON-MAGICAL USES: Liquorice root is chewed to help against a range of lung complaints, from coughs and bronchitis to asthma. It also strengthens the immune system to deal with allergies and after taking strong traditional medicines such as antibiotics and steroids. Liquorice is drunk as a strong tea to detoxify. Chewing on liquorice can raise your blood pressure briefly, so it should not be taken by those who suffer from high blood pressure. Due to its strong, sweet flavor, it can be used to mask the bitter taste of other medicinal herbs.

OFTEN COMBINED WITH: Wild garlic, when dealing with the dead in magic spells. Or liquorice and wild garlic are put on the altar, then eaten together when trying to contact ancestors.

SPELL

If you wish to make contact with your ancestors, rub a black candle with liquorice oil or a liquorice root. Light it, then place a photo of the ancestor (or their name on a piece of paper if lacking a photo) in front of the candle. Visualize yourself with them and start talking to them.

Water ☆ West

CELERY

PLANET: Mercury

DEITY: Apollo, God of Poetry and Music

MAGICAL USES: Mental and psychic powers, weight loss

NON-MAGICAL USES: A stick of celery can be applied directly to the skin to treat fungal infections. Eaten or drunk as tea, celery will help clear up skin problems and stimulate the circulation and blood flow, such as to bring on menstruation. Celery seeds are sometimes chewed to ease stress and nervousness, and may lower blood pressure.

OFTEN COMBINED WITH: Thyme, to increase knowledge and concentration when studying. You can add them to a baked dish or salad, or just keep both in your study.

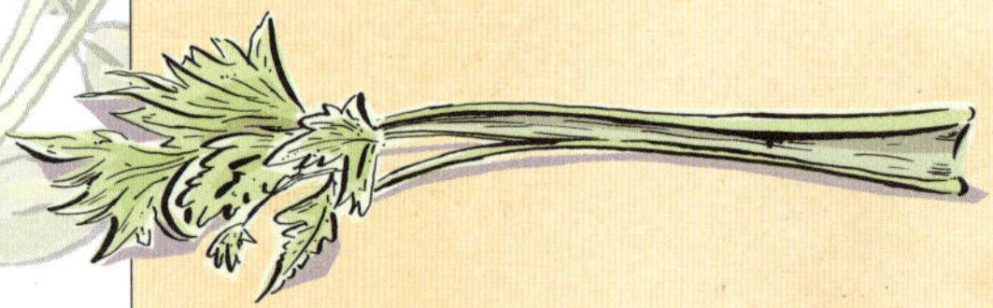

SPELL

When dieting, each morning make a pentagram shape with five stalks of celery while imagining yourself slim and healthy; eat one stalk before each meal or snack.

CUCUMBER

PLANET: Moon

DEITY: Hera, Goddess of Purification and Marriage

MAGICAL USES: Chastity, prosperity

NON-MAGICAL USES: Refreshing to the mind and body, cucumber can be applied to sunburnt skin to heal it, bee stings to reduce swelling, and to aching feet to soothe them.

OFTEN COMBINED WITH: Valerian, and eaten whenever you are away from your lover to keep you both true to each other and the relationship peaceful and strong.

SPELL

Push five copper coins into a cucumber (space them evenly) to bring prosperity to your family. Place the cucumber by your front door; replace when the cucumber gets flabby.

LEMON

Planet: Pluto

Deity: Juno, Goddess of Fidelity and Protection

Magical uses: Anti-negativity, friendship, exams, longevity

Non-magical uses: A cut lemon rubbed on the skin is used to treat varicose veins and hemorrhoids as well as cellulite. Lemon peel is eaten to ease upset stomachs. Lemon is great for boosting the immune system, especially in winter, due to its high vitamin C content, and lemon diluted in water can be gargled to ease sore throats. Lemon essential oil is refreshing and helps with concentration—you can use it in an aromatherapy burner.

Often combined with: Cardamom in food, to promote friendship.

SPELL

To remove negativity from the home, quarter a lemon and place one slice into each corner of the main room of your home (usually living room). The lemon will soak up negative energy and may go black. Remove when black or moldy.

POPPY

Planet: Moon

Deity: Demeter, Goddess of the Harvest

Magical uses: Divination, fertility, sleep

Non-magical uses: Boiled in liquid (usually wine), poppy seeds can be drunk to ease stomach upsets. They give great energy and are often eaten by athletes before a long day's training. A syrup or tea can be made from poppy petals to promote sleep.

Often combined with: Jasmine tea, and drunk before dream magic (see Chapter 1, page 17).

SPELL

To see what the future brings, throw a handful of poppy seeds onto a small fire (such as in a cauldron, or on a piece of charcoal). Inhale the smoke and ask the deities to show you the answer to your question.

Chapter 6

Herbal Spells

I love writing my own spells and have done so even before I joined a coven—so I have been writing spells for more than half my life. All the spells in this chapter have worked successfully for either myself or someone I know personally, so they have a good chance of working for you too.

I have tried to show how much variety there is in herbal magic spells by providing different types of spell (knot and candle spells, witch bottles, baths, etc) for a variety of magical intentions, from prosperity, work, and money to love, sex, and friendship to protection, justice, health, and wisdom.

Unless you are an experienced witch, I would recommend reading Chapter 1, The Basics of Herbal Magic, before reading this chapter. It will give you a better idea of how magic works, thus making your spells more powerful.

Feel free to experiment too, and change the spells a little to suit your own circumstances and needs (see Chapter 8, page 144).

Prosperity Spells

Prosperity spells are those that make your life better and easier in general, rather than doing something specific, such as increasing money, eliminating debt, drawing more customers to your business, or getting rid of an annoying co-worker, for example, although a prosperity spell may do some or all of those things, too.

Think of a prosperity spell as one asking the universe/spirit/God or whatever higher power you believe in to make things better, but rather than simply praying, you do something about it yourself by gathering prosperity-inducing ingredients and performing a spell to attract prosperity energy.

I have included money spells in this section (see pages 91–94), because they are always in demand. However, in many ways, prosperity spells are safer than money spells, especially for beginners. This is because with prosperity spells you don't ask for large sums of money, which may seem greedy to the deities, and don't have to specify that you do not want the money to come from "bad" sources, such as an inheritance. You are simply asking the universe to make your life a success and you a prosperous person.

Prosperity spells can be done at any time, though as you are trying to increase your wealth and success, the best time for these spells is when things in nature are on the increase, too—so, for example, during a waxing moon, at harvest times, or at dawn as the sun rises in the sky.

"There's fennel for you, and columbines; there's rue for you; and here's some for me; we may call it herb of grace O'Sundays."
Hamlet, William Shakespeare (1564–1616)

MUSTARD SEED SPELL FOR PROSPERITY

SPELL INGREDIENTS

- ☆ Tiger's eye gemstone
- ☆ Handful of salt
- ☆ 12 mustard seeds

SPELL WORK

On the day before a new moon, bury the tiger's eye gem in the salt. The day after the new moon, take the gem out and clean it by washing it in a clear stream or river, or if that is not possible, under running water in a sink. Hold the tiger's eye and the mustard seeds in your left hand (the left guides your intuition), and ask the universe to guide you toward prosperity with the help of the mustard seeds. Eat one mustard seed every day until the full moon.

STAR ANISE CANDLE SPELL FOR PROSPERITY

SPELL INGREDIENTS

- ☆ Star anise
- ☆ Green or gold candle

SPELL WORK

Stick some star anise onto a candle; if the candle is soft, you should be able to just push the star anise onto the candle, but if not, you may need to use a drop of wax from another green or gold candle to place each star anise seed onto the spell candle. Light this candle before you do anything prosperity-related, such as going to job interviews, talking to your bank manager, or paying bills, to boost your prospects.

HERBAL DUST SPELL FOR PROSPERITY

SPELL INGREDIENTS

- ☆ Mix of dried prosperity herbs (whatever you have around, such as basil, bay, red clover, thyme, etc.)
- ☆ Baby powder

SPELL WORK

Mix the herbs and the baby powder while saying the following nine times:

"With the passing of time—
prosperity will be mine!"

Use the powder to dust your feet each morning before you put on your socks and shoes.

FIRE SPELL FOR PROSPERITY

SPELL INGREDIENTS

- ☆ Cauldron, fireplace, or other fire safe place
- ☆ 3 leaves each of camomile and basil
- ☆ Earth (preferably from near where you work)

SPELL WORK

Make a small fire in your cauldron or fireplace. Watch the flame and feel its warmth while visualizing your life going well and you being prosperous. Drop the camomile and basil leaves into the fire and add a sprinkle of earth. Say the following:

"I ask the earth to nourish me in my endeavors
I ask the powers that watch over me to bless and keep me
As I will it, so mote it be!"

Add more earth until you have extinguished the flame. The spell is now done and you can discard the earth/ash mix if you like, but this would also make an ideal nourishing soil for your next batch of home-grown magical herbs!

COPPER COIN SPELL FOR SUCCESS

SPELL INGREDIENTS

- ☆ 9 copper coins, such as pennies
- ☆ Small symbols of success, such as the car and hotel figures from Monopoly, a picture of a safe, a photo of a yacht, a gem stone, etc—whatever prosperity means to you
- ☆ Pinch of cardamom
- ☆ Rosemary oil

SPELL WORK

Place the coins in a clockwise circle on your altar or on a table in a quiet place where the spell can be left undisturbed. Place a symbol of prosperity on each. Put the pinch of cardamom in the middle of the circle to attract the prosperity energies, and finally draw a circle outside the coin circle with the rosemary oil, drizzling it counter clockwise (to ward off negative energies and those who do not wish you to be prosperous). Leave this arrangement in place until you see definite improvements in your prosperity.

Money Spells

Money spells are somewhat tricky, and it is important to word them carefully and correctly. If you do not, the spell may still work and you may get your money, but your newly acquired finances might have a negative source, such as an inheritance from your much-loved aunt, or a payoff after an accident. Similarly to what I say in the Home and Work section of this chapter (page 106–109), you also need to be realistic, because although spells increase the probability of something happening, they do not make anything certain.

For example, if you performed a money spell and asked for a million in cash or a lottery win, your odds would increase slightly—but they would still be extremely small, even if your chances of winning were doubled. Whereas if you performed a money spell and asked for just enough to cover your bills, there would be many potential sources for that amount (assuming that your bills are much less than one million, of course!). For instance, you might get a raise, find a large-denomination note in the street, or a friend may pay you back for a loan you had totally forgotten about!

"Yes, in the poor man's garden grow
Far more than herbs and flowers
Kind thoughts, contentment, peace of mind
And joy for weary hours."
Mary Howitt (1799–1888)

THYME CANDLE SPELL FOR MORE MONEY

SPELL INGREDIENTS

- ☆ Green or gold candle
- ☆ Dried thyme

SPELL WORK

Inscribe some money signs (such as $, £) onto your candle. Light it every Thursday during daylight hours, then sprinkle some thyme into the flame (be careful, the thyme may still burn when it falls to the ground, so this spell is best performed in the kitchen sink or a similar fireproof place). Do this until your finances improve—but don't get greedy!

PENNYROYAL AND CINNAMON SPELL TO PAY OFF DEBTS

SPELL INGREDIENTS

- ☆ Green candle
- ☆ Gold cloth
- ☆ Pennyroyal leaf
- ☆ 3 pumpkin seeds
- ☆ 3 copper coins (such as pennies)
- ☆ Cinnamon stick
- ☆ Gold chain

SPELL WORK

On a Thursday during the waxing moon, light the green candle. Spread the cloth before it and place all the other spell ingredients onto the cloth while you imagine being free of all your money troubles. Fold the cloth, with all the other things in it, into a little pouch, sealing it with green wax from the candle while saying:

"My life is tragic
I need some money magic!
Pennyroyal do your will
Let me pay the bill!
I also add the pumpkin seed
To fulfill my financial need
Cinnamon stick
Do the trick!"

Make a little hole in two corners of the pouch and thread the gold chain through it. Wear this money talisman against your skin every day until your debts or other need for money lessens.

PATCHOULI AND BASIL SPELL FOR WEALTH

SPELL INGREDIENTS

- ☆ Patchouli incense
- ☆ Dried basil

SPELL WORK

Light the patchouli incense while thinking about how you are going to make money. Gather the ashes from the incense and mix with crushed dried basil leaves. Go to the top of a hill or high building and throw the mixture into the wind on a sunny day while saying:

"I have need for money
So may life may be happy and sunny
Lord and Lady don't let me despair
I give this offering to the air
Bring wealth and money to me
As I ask it, so mote it be!"

BASIL AND BAY SPELL FOR FINDING THE MONEY YOU NEED

SPELL INGREDIENTS

- ☆ Coins
- ☆ Cauldron or large black pot
- ☆ 5 basil leaves
- ☆ 5 bay leaves

SPELL WORK

At dawn, make a circle on the ground with the coins, large enough to place you cauldron on it. Fill the cauldron with water (rain water is best, but tap water will do). Swirl the water clockwise while chanting:

"I pray, I chant
Money and success me grant
Lord and Lady help me see
Where the money I need may be!"

Drop the basil and bay leaves into the swirling water in the cauldron and watch how they move and what forms they make. From the shapes and figures, you will be able to divine how you can make the money you need.

BASIL SPELL FOR A COMFORTABLE LIFE

SPELL INGREDIENTS

- ☆ Large basil leaf
- ☆ A cash note (it doesn't have to be a large denomination)

SPELL WORK

Kiss the basil leaf, then place it on the note. Fold the note four times while saying:

"I ask for enough to live comfortably
I am a good person, I deserve this money
I do not ask for much
Just enough to pay bills, have food and such!"

Keep the note with the basil in it in your wallet.

PENNYROYAL KNOT SPELL FOR MONEY AND SUCCESS

SPELL INGREDIENTS

- ☆ 3 long stalks of pennyroyal

SPELL WORK

Take one stalk, and make three knots in it. While tying each knot, say:

"By knot one, my spell's begun
By knot two, good work I'll do
By knot three, money comes to me!"

Take the second stalk and again make three knots in it, saying:

"By knot four, opportunity knocks at my door
By knot five, success is my life
By knot six, this spell is fixed!"

Take the last of the three stalks and while again making three knots, say:

"By knot seven, success will be given
By knot eight, my need is great
By knot nine, these things are mine!"

Love, Fertility, and Sex Spells

Love spells and money spells are probably the most popular magic, and those I get asked for the most. Love, fertility, and sex spells can be particularly tricky, as it is important not to go against the free will of a person you fancy and want to fall in love with you; forcing someone to love you would be breaking their will, and thus black magic. Most witches will refuse to do this, or help others in doing such magic. That doesn't mean that you cannot perform any love spells at all, though! There are three types of love spells that are perfectly fine to do, and also tend to work better than those ones involving forcing another person to fall in love with you.

Love spells that are fine to do

- General love spells that bring love into your life from whereever it may be—for these to work, you need to be open to love coming from anywhere, including the mailman, the shop assistant at the grocery store, or the colleague sitting next to you.
- Spells that make existing feelings stronger. These are good when you are too shy to ask out a guy you already know through a sports club, or have a long-term friend you realize you'd like more than a friendship with. They can also be spells you perform in the early parts of a love relationship, such as after a few dates. These types of spell will *not* work if the person targeted doesn't want a love relationship with you, the magic will just move things along and will make you and the other person more willing to progress, (such as by asking the other person out).
- Spells that have a caveat, such as saying "And it harm none/for the good of all", "if it be the will of the deities and [other person]", or something similar. This will negate any egotistical feelings you may have put into the spell, and make sure that your magic doesn't break the target's free will.

Spells for finding love

FLOWER SPELL FOR LOVE

SPELL INGREDIENTS

- ☆ 5 ROSE PETALS (PINK FOR ROMANTIC LOVE, RED FOR SEXUAL LOVE)
- ☆ 5 JASMINE FLOWERS (YOU CAN TAKE THE DRIED FLOWER OUT OF JASMINE TEA IF YOU CANNOT GET FRESH)
- ☆ BERGAMOT OIL
- ☆ SMALL BOTTLE

SPELL WORK

The day after a new moon, put all the ingredients together into the bottle; make sure you have enough oil to cover the rose petals and flowers. Shake this every day while thinking about the qualities your ideal lover has. On the full moon, your love magic oil will be ready: dab a little on your breast and neck whenever you go out or do any activity where you may meet your future loved one!

POWER-OF-THREE SPELL FOR LOVE

SPELL INGREDIENTS

- ☆ PINK CANDLE
- ☆ SEASHELL (PREFERABLY ONE YOU PICKED UP YOURSELF AT THE SHORE)
- ☆ 1 ROSEHIP
- ☆ VANILLA POD
- ☆ PINCH OF CINNAMON

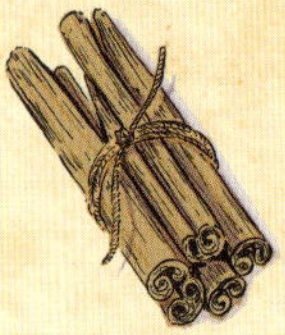

SPELL WORK

Light the candle and pass the seashell through the flame three times, each time saying:

"By the power of three, love here may be!".

Spend some time gazing into the candle flame and imagining yourself attracting the ideal partner. Place the rosehip into the shell, scrape the vanilla pod into the shell, and sprinkle cinnamon over it. As you do each of these tasks, again say:

"By the power of three, love here may be!".

Bring the seashell and its contents to the seashore and toss it into the sea (or if that is not possible, a river), so that the water deities may take the offering and bring you love in return.

RASPBERRY ROSE BATH SPELL FOR LOVE

SPELL INGREDIENTS

- ☆ 34 FL OZ (1 LITER) RASPBERRY JUICE
- ☆ ROSE PETALS

SPELL WORK

Draw a warm bath and add the raspberry juice to the running water. Get into the bath, then sprinkle the rose petals in a clockwise motion around you. As you do so, imagine yourself being filled with love and attracting love from others. Do not rinse or use soap afterward (you can take a shower first to get clean if needed).

SPELLS FOR STRENGTHENING LOVE AND MOVING FRIENDSHIP TO LOVE

SPELL FOR LOVE TO FLOWER

SPELL INGREDIENTS

- ☆ ONE ONION
- ☆ RED PEN
- ☆ 3 CARDAMOM SEEDS
- ☆ SOIL AND POT

SPELL WORK

Write the name of the person you love around the root part of a whole onion with a red pen. Plant the onion in the pot together with three cardamom seeds and place the pot on a windowsill, facing the direction of his or her home. Smile at the pot every day and say:

"Our love grows as the roots of this onion take hold
Our love will be strong like the stem of this plant
Our love will flower like this onion!".

When the onion flowers, take the flower and use it in a dish you feed your loved one or, if this is not possible, drop it in the path of the other person so they walk over it.

INCENSE SPELL FOR FUN AND PASSION

SPELL INGREDIENTS

- ☆ Sandalwood incense
- ☆ A photo of the two of you together, smiling
- ☆ Patchouli incense

SPELL WORK

Light the sandalwood incense and imagine content, peaceful times together while you waft the incense smoke around the photo. Then light the patchouli incense and imagine things moving from peaceful to sexy and fun, while you again waft the incense smoke around the photo.

SPELL FOR RED-HOT LOVE

SPELL INGREDIENTS

- ☆ 5 blue violets
- ☆ 5 red peppercorns
- ☆ Water: holy water is ideal, but spring water will do

SPELL WORK

Drop the violets and peppercorns in the holy water and let the moon shine on it (a full moon is ideal). Then place two of the violets and peppercorns under your pillow, two under the other person's, and one in the middle (or halfway between his home and yours if you do not share a home yet). Say:

"Violets so blue, our love will be true
"Peppercorn red, we'll only be in each other's bed!"

Spells to reawaken love and lust after troubled times

JASMINE SPELL: TO GET BACK TOGETHER WITH A LOVER

SPELL INGREDIENTS

- ☆ 2 WHITE CANDLES
- ☆ JASMINE OIL
- ☆ 1 BLUE CANDLE

SPELL WORK

Carve your name into one of the white candles, and the name of the lover you want to reconcile with into the other white candle. Rub jasmine oil into the blue candle. Light both white candles, then tip them and hold them close together until the two flames become one. Light the blue candle with the joined flame. While doing so, say:

"Be gone hostility
Come here, tranquility!
If there is still love between us, let it be!"

THYME AND NUTMEG SPELL TO REAWAKEN ROMANCE

SPELL INGREDIENTS

- ☆ 1 RED APPLE
- ☆ 2 CHERRIES
- ☆ 3 SPRINGS OF THYME
- ☆ 4 PINCHES OF POWDERED NUTMEG
- ☆ 5 DROPS OF ROSE OIL

SPELL WORK

Cut the apple in half and carefully take out the middle, so you have two little bowls. Split the ingredients between the two apple halves and mix them together with your left index finger while saying:

"I stir this magic [PARTNER'S NAME] *and romance will reawaken!*
I stir the love
As below, so above!".

Place the two apple halves back together and bury the apple into the ground near where you live (ideally in your garden). As the apple gets reabsorbed into Mother Earth, so the love between you and your partner will reawaken.

PARSLEY AND ALMOND PRAYER SPELL FOR CONCEPTION

SPELL INGREDIENTS

- ☆ Parsley
- ☆ Almond oil

SPELL WORK

Finely chop the parsley and mix with the almond oil. The male partner should rub the oil onto the female's stomach in a clockwise direction while both chanting in unison:

"Pink for a girl and blue for a boy
Wee one, you will bring such joy
Fill up this womb with a baby
For sure, no doubt, no maybe
We are prepared, we are ready
We hold so much love, our life is steady
Tonight with child we'll be
As we will it, so mote it be!"

MANDRAKE AND CINNAMON SPELL FOR FERTILITY

SPELL INGREDIENTS

- ☆ Whole mandrake root
- ☆ Cinnamon stick
- ☆ Carrot
- ☆ Green wool

SPELL WORK

Tie together the mandrake root, cinnamon stick, and carrot with the green woolen thread. Wind the thread around the three objects nine times, each time, saying:

"Goddess of fertility, bring the spark of life to me."

Leave the bundle under the bed or wherever you usually make love. Throw it away when you have conceived or replace it before the carrot becomes limp if necessary.

FENNEL SPELL FOR EASY PREGNANCY

SPELL INGREDIENTS

- ☆ Egg shell
- ☆ Sprig of fennel
- ☆ Blue ribbon

SPELL WORK

Carefully blow out an egg so that you end up with an intact shell with a little hole at the top. Place the sprig of fennel in the little hole while praying to a Mother Goddess, such as Brigit or Cybele, for an easy conception, pregnancy, and delivery. Tie the blue ribbon around the egg carefully and place the beribboned egg in the north side of your home.

SPELL FOR SPICE IN THE BEDROOM

SPELL INGREDIENTS

- ☆ Chili
- ☆ Cinnamon
- ☆ Honey

SPELL WORK

Mix the three ingredients together while saying:

"Sex and virility
Come to us, we want thee!"

Eat a little of the mixture, feed some to your partner, and dab a little at the base of your spine before sex.

CHILI AND PARSLEY SPELL FOR INTIMACY

SPELL INGREDIENTS

- ☆ 1 sheet of red paper
- ☆ Glue
- ☆ Chili
- ☆ Parsley
- ☆ Red peppercorns

SPELL WORK

On the red paper, outline a male shape with glue, then sprinkle the chili on it. Next, outline a female shape over the male and sprinkle parsley on that. Frame the two shapes by gluing peppercorns in a heart shape around them. Keep this magical artwork in your bedroom to keep the bond between you fiery and true.

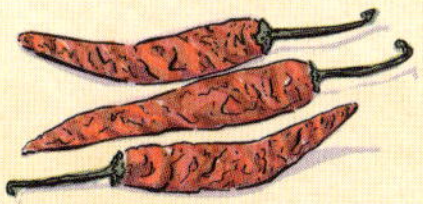

Friendship and Relationship Spells

Friendship spells and love spells are very close to one another—after all, a love relationship often starts off as a friendship, and many couples see their relationship as a friendship with an extra dimension. Thus, you can usually adapt a love spell to serve as a friendship spell and the other way around, simply by using a different magical herb, colored candle, or some such. As with love spells, it would be black magic and wrong to force someone to be your friend, and no good magic will make you one of the in-crowd if they are bullies and simply don't like you, or if you will not fit in with that group. But a friendship spell will make the in-crowd willing to consider you as a friend—you'll have to do the rest—or it can help you get back in the in-crowd if an argument got you excluded.

When performing a friendship or relationship spell, first think about you and the other person and try and see things from their point of view, especially when there is bad blood or there has been an argument. There is no point performing a spell for peaceful relations with the in-laws if you growl at them each time you see them!

"Friends, books, a garden, and perhaps his pen,
Delightful industry enjoy'd at home,
And Nature, in her cultivated trim
Dress'd to his taste, inviting him abroad—
Can he want occupation who has these?"
William Cowper (1731–1800)

VALERIAN AND LAVENDER SPELL TO FIND MORE FRIENDS

SPELL INGREDIENTS

- ☆ Beeswax or yellow candle
- ☆ Small valerian leaves
- ☆ Lavender flowers

SPELL WORK

Ideally, make your own beeswax candle and add some valerian leaves and lavender flowers to the wax as you pour or dip the candle. If you cannot make your own candle, get a plain beeswax or yellow candle and some clear wax. Carefully make a little indentation into the beeswax candle, put a valerian leaf into it, push the wax you took off the candle over the leaf and seal with the clear wax. Do the same for the lavender flower and continue until you are happy with the amount of leaves and flowers on the candle (the amount will depend on the candle; don't overdo it, as too much will impair the burning of the candle). Burn this candle for a few minutes every day while you pray to deities you like and/or are associated with friendship and relationships, such as Artemis, Juno, or Ganesha, to bring you new or more fun friends.

SPELL TO FORM NEW FRIENDSHIPS

SPELL INGREDIENTS

- ☆ Sprig of lavender
- ☆ Yellow candle

SPELL WORK

Gently push the sprig of lavender into the yellow candle about ¼ in (.75 cm) from the top. Light the candle and chant the following until the wax melts enough for the lavender sprig to fall, which is when the magic is done:

"I am starting a new life
I want no trouble, no strife
Friends I'll make anew
Maybe not many, but a good few!"

Then extinguish the candle.

CARDAMOM SPELL TO TURN AN ADVERSARY INTO A FRIEND

SPELL INGREDIENTS

- ☆ Photo of a person who dislikes you whom you want to befriend (if you cannot get a photo, take a piece of paper they have touched and write their name on it)
- ☆ Cardamom seed

SPELL WORK

Just after a full moon, take the photo of the person and rub the cardamom seed over it while chanting:

"You don't like me
That is not how I want it to be
I'll turn you into a friend
By this spell's end!"

Do this every day for a lunar cycle, and by the next full moon, the spell will be done.

CLOVE SPELL TO RESTORE FRIENDSHIP

SPELL INGREDIENTS

- ☆ Whole clove
- ☆ Photo of you and your friend

SPELL WORK

After you have had a fight with a friend, or if you feel someone is trying to break you up, do the following spell to restore the friendship. Place the clove onto the photo and say:

"Let this clove
Take the anger from above
I don't want a dip
In our friendship!"

Then remove the clove, break it in two, and throw it into the air while saying:

"As this clove is broken and thrown away
Negativity be gone, friendship stay!"

CARDAMOM SPELL TO GET A FRIEND TO CONTACT YOU

SPELL INGREDIENTS

- ☆ Cardamom seed
- ☆ Photo of the friend
- ☆ Phone

SPELL WORK

To get a friend to contact you, rub a cardamom seed over a photo of the friend or something the friend has given you, then rub it over your phone, and chew and swallow the cardamom seed while visualizing the friend phoning you.

LEMON BALM AND LAVENDER SPELL TO KEEP THE PEACE

SPELL INGREDIENTS

- ☆ Lemon balm
- ☆ Lavender
- ☆ Honey
- ☆ White container, such as a small porcelain bowl or white painted bottle

SPELL WORK

Place all three ingredients in the container. Leave open and place somewhere the family gathers, or in the meeting room at work. This will ensure everything stays peaceful and amicable. Replace if the mixture gets dirty or it gathers dust.

Spells for Home and Work

The key to performing spells for finding a new home or selling an old one, as well as finding well-paid work or getting a promotion, is to be realistic about your expectations. There is no point casting a spell to find a seven-bedroom, five-bathroom home with room for a pony if you currently live in a basic rented apartment with no savings. If you were to perform the spell regardless, you may find a listing for the house, but the price would be too high for you to afford; or if you could afford the price, the house would be out of reach, halfway around the world.

The same goes for work spells, such as those to help you find your ideal job—although there is a subtle difference, in that a seemingly unattainable work goal may be reachable if you really, truly want it and are willing to work for it and look long term. So if you are an unskilled worker who didn't graduate from school and your dream job is to be a professor of theoretical physics, will magic get you your goal? No, not by itself, but it can help give you the confidence to go back to school, and the willpower and patience to work long hours for many years until that dream becomes a realistic goal.

"In the nice bee, what sense so subtly true
From pois'nous herbs extracts the healing dew?"
Alexander Pope (1688–1744)

Spells for Finding a New Home

HERB AND CRYSTAL FULL MOON SPELL FOR A PERFECT HOME

SPELL INGREDIENTS

- ☆ Red clover flower
- ☆ Clear quartz crystal
- ☆ Bay leaf
- ☆ White thread

SPELL WORK

On a full moon, place the red clover flower on the crystal and wrap them in the bay leaf. Secure the parcel with the white thread while chanting:

"I ask the Moon Goddess so round
A new home for me shall be found
Nice rooms, and clean ground
Happiness and comfort abound!"

Carry the parcel with you when talking to agents or viewing houses.

CITRONELLA SPELL TO FIND THE BEST HOME

SPELL INGREDIENTS

- ☆ All the listings of the homes you are trying to decide between
- ☆ 1 citronella leaf per listing

SPELL WORK

Place all the listings on your altar or, if you do not have one, on a table where they can be left undisturbed for several days. Place a citronella leaf (the fresher the better) on each listing and say:

"Citronella make loud and clear
Is our home far, or is it near?
Please tell me where we should dwell
Let us find a cheap sell!"

Repeat this chant every day at two or three separate times during the day. Pay close attention to the citronella leaves; if some dry up or go moldy, disregard the listings that they're resting on. If the citronella leaf blows off one or two house details, definitely make those houses your top priority for viewing!

Spells for selling a home

HERB-WATER SPELL FOR SELLING A HOUSE

SPELL INGREDIENTS

- 3 crushed bay leaves
- 5 basil leaves
- Cinnamon stick
- Small handful of red clover (the green parts)
- Pinch of nutmeg

SPELL WORK

Add everything together in a pan and cover with water. Bring to the boil and lightly simmer, letting the steam waft through the house to be sold. Keep simmering until the water is reduced to half. Place everything into a bottle or jar and use to wash windowsills, door jambs, and fence posts before a viewing.

CINNAMON SPELL TO WELCOME BUYERS

SPELL INGREDIENTS

- Cinnamon incense
- Green paint

SPELL WORK

When trying to sell your home, mix some cinnamon into a pot of green paint and paint your front door with it. If you are unable to paint the door, sprinkle some cinnamon onto a green welcome mat.

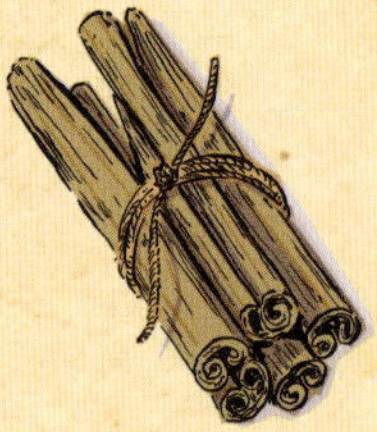

Spells for finding work

HERBAL PENTAGRAM SPELL TO FIND A GREAT JOB

SPELL INGREDIENTS

- ☆ Green paper
- ☆ Gold marker pen
- ☆ Handful of Irish Moss
- ☆ 5 buckthorn leaves

SPELL WORK

Cut the green paper into a pentagram shape. On each of the five points, use the gold marker to write one thing you'd like your new job to offer (such as having your own office, being close to home, allowing you to be creative, having a nice boss, or being with an ethical company). Sprinkle the Irish Moss in the middle and place one buckthorn leaf on each point. Visualize your pentagram while you are waiting at reception for job interviews and before reading the job adverts in the paper.

TARRAGON AND THYME BUSINESS CARD SPELL

SPELL INGREDIENTS

- ☆ White candle
- ☆ Small piece of white cardboard/heavy paper
- ☆ Black pen
- ☆ Sprig of tarragon
- ☆ Sprig of thyme

SPELL WORK

Light the white candle. Cut the cardboard to business-card size, then design it to look like your business card for your ideal job (you can do this on the computer too, if you have one, and a printer). Rub the card with the tarragon and thyme sprigs while thinking about the small ways you are going to work toward your goal of the ideal job (looking at job adverts, furthering your education, networking, etc). Pass the herb sprigs through the flame of the candle slowly until they start smoldering. Let the smoke waft around the business card; watch the smoke while saying a prayer to your favorite deities to help you get that ideal job.

Spells for Justice and Protection

When performing a justice or protection spell, keep in mind that even though the spell may be successful, you might never know. For example, if a protection spell worked and you did not get burgled or assaulted on the way home, it would be impossible to decide whether this was because of the spell, other measures you may have taken, or even just due to pure luck. In the case of a justice spell in a court case, the final judge's decision may only go half in your favor, but that may just be the outcome of the case; if you performed a justice spell to get justice in a bad situation at work, for example, it may seem as if nothing had happened to the work colleague you had a problem with, when in fact he/she was punished behind closed doors.

Most justice spells here were written to help with court cases, but that doesn't mean this is the only time they can be used. In many cases in which justice is needed, the case never gets to court, or indeed the situation may not be a legal one—it could be unfair treatment at work, or bullying at school. The spells in this section can be used for all such situations, with minor adaptations of the chant if necessary.

"If one way be better than another, that you may be sure is Nature's way."
Aristotle (384–322 BCE)

Justice Spells

EYEBRIGHT SPELL TO SEE JUSTICE DONE

SPELL INGREDIENTS

- ☆ Black candle
- ☆ Eyebright

SPELL WORK

Light the black candle on your altar and visualize the bad person being fairly judged or court case being resolved. Sprinkle eyebright in a square shape in an counter clockwise motion around the candle while chanting:

"Holy Father, Goddess Divine
I asked justice at your sacred shrine
Please let the judge hear
Make his mind open, lend me his ear
Make the judgment fair
I ask, as I finish this square!"

The magic starts working immediately and will finish when the situation is resolved.

DILL AND RICE SPELL FOR A FAIR SAY IN COURT

SPELL INGREDIENTS

- ☆ Orange pen
- ☆ White paper
- ☆ Orange bell pepper
- ☆ Dill
- ☆ Rice
- ☆ Blue candle

SPELL WORK

Using orange pen, write the names of each of the people involved in the court case on separate pieces of paper. Cut the pepper in half and remove the seeds. Place the pieces of paper inside the pepper, starting with the person you think is the most correct in the case (if there is one who is more correct than the other). Sprinkle each piece with dill. Fill the pepper with rice (to symbolize everyone having their fair say in court), light the blue candle, take some wax from it, and use it to seal the pepper. Bury it outside your property. While you can perform this spell any time during court proceedings, it is best to do it as soon as possible, so that Mother Earth has time to work her magic as the pepper disintegrates.

CLOVE AND VALERIAN SPELL TO TRANSFORM BAD BEHAVIOR

SPELL INGREDIENTS

- ☆ Black candle
- ☆ Cloves
- ☆ White candle
- ☆ Valerian (flowers if possible, but the leaves will do)

SPELL WORK

Just after the full moon, carve the name of the person who has been causing you trouble (noisy neighbors, or a difficult boss, etc) into a black candle. Lay down the cloves around the candle in a circle counter clockwise. (Make sure you do this where the candle in the circle can be left undisturbed for a while, such as on a windowsill or put the candle and cloves on a plate so you can move it into a cupboard during the day.) Light the candle every day for a few minutes, thinking about the bad behavior of the person lessening. On the new moon, replace the black candle with a white one, again with the person's name carved on it, and this time make a clockwise circle around the candle with the valerian. Light it every day until the full moon, thinking about relations between the two of you becoming civil and nice. If necessary, you can repeat this spell for several months, although you should see signs of things getting better after one month.

Protection spells

GARLIC AND LAVENDER SPELL TO WARD OFF NEGATIVITY

SPELL INGREDIENTS

- ☆ Wild garlic
- ☆ Lavender
- ☆ Wire or blue-colored string

SPELL WORK

If you have visitors coming who may be negatively inclined toward you (maybe in-laws who don't like you, the landlord, or jealous friends)—make a braid with wild garlic and lavender (you will likely need some wire or blue-colored string to keep it together) and hang it in your kitchen to ward off negativity. If you cannot find wild garlic, instead buy ready-made braids of white garlic from the grocery store.

MANDRAKE AND ROSEMARY PROTECTION SPELL FOR TRAVELERS

SPELL INGREDIENTS

- Mandrake root
- Rosemary essential oil
- Salt

SPELL WORK

Rub the mandrake root with rosemary oil and sprinkle with salt. Hold it up to the sun and say:

"I ask the Sun God to protect my man
So he may return safely as soon as he can
Any dangers keep away
Strong and healthy he'll stay!"

Keep the mandrake root wrapped in a piece of clothing belonging to the person you are protecting and leave it where it won't be disturbed. When the person you are protecting is safely back home, bury the root in the soil. This spell was originally designed to protect soldiers going off to war during the Hundred Year War, but can be used to protect anyone who is traveling.

HERBAL WITCH BOTTLE FOR GOOD HEALTH

SPELL INGREDIENTS

- Blue candle
- Clear glass bottle
- Sprig of rosemary
- Cumin
- Feverfew or eucalyptus leaves
- Vinegar

SPELL WORK

Light the blue candle. Fill up the bottle with the rosemary, cumin, and feverfew or eucalyptus. As you do so, chant:

"Rosemary divine
In this witch bottle of mine
Seeds of cumin
Protect me from sin
Healthy I'll stay
Content and gay!"

Fill the bottle up with vinegar and seal it with wax from the blue candle. Keep this jar near the front door of your home.

SAGE SPELL FOR HAPPINESS AND PROTECTION

SPELL INGREDIENTS

- 5 sage sprigs
- Black thread
- Brown thread

SPELL WORK

Bunch the sage sprigs together, then wind the black and brown threads around the sage alternating like a spiral, so that only the top of the sage is showing—the result will look a bit like a thin magic wand. Hold this in your right hand (or left, if you are left-handed) and walk clockwise around your home while chanting:

"Bless this home
So happiness may roam
Protection I ask for
Safe and secure, forever more!"

Hang the sage wand upside down in a dry place until the sage has completely dried. Then light the sage wand and repeat the ritual so it smolders and the smoke gets into every corner and crevice. Extinguish the wand when you are done... and keep it somewhere safe so you can repeat this spell as needed.

MUSTARD AND NETTLE SPELL FOR PROTECTING THE HOME

SPELL INGREDIENTS

- Grainy mustard
- Nettle (the stingier the better)
- Rose thorns
- Small tin (if you cannot find a small storage tin, you may re-use a well cleaned jar of sweetcorn or similar)

SPELL WORK

Add all the ingredients to the tin while saying:

"I ask for protection
Of all my home, not just this section
Mustard seed
Do your deed!"

Place the tin in the middle of your home in a dark place (such as under a floorboard or at the back of a closet). Leave it there for the whole time you live there.

Health and Luck Spells

The health spells written here are to be performed on oneself, but of course you can change the wording slightly so they apply to a friend or loved one. You can also do health spells for someone you do not know personally—for example, covens have healing circles (similar to Christian prayer circles) where a High Priestess can ask for healing for one of her coven members from a group of covens, some of whose members may never have met each other.

Spells should not be performed on another person without their knowledge. As discussed before, this would be breaking their free will and thus be black magic. Even when doing a simple healing spell, which you may think can do no harm, one should ask permission from the sick person first; they may not be comfortable with magic being performed for them because of their religion or scientific views, or they may be at peace with their illness and just want it to run its course. And if a luck spell is targeted at a specific event, such as to pass a test, it is important that you also work in other ways to achieve this goal—don't just perform the spell and then sit back and watch TV. Go study!

*"Why should a man die while sage grows in the garden?
For herbs bring health and peace."*
Old Chinese proverb

OREGANO AND ALLSPICE BATH SPELL FOR HEALING

SPELL INGREDIENTS

- ☆ Oregano
- ☆ Allspice
- ☆ Blue cheesecloth

SPELL WORK

Place the oregano and allspice in the middle of the blue cheesecloth. Tie the four corners of the cloth to make a pouch. Run a warm bath and place the pouch into the bath water. As you get into the bath, imagine yourself encased in a blue bubble of healing. When you are ready to get out of the bath, open the spice pouch, then take the plug out of the bath. Watch the water and spices drain down the plughole and as you do so, imagine all the sickness, pain, and discomfort leaving your body.

CAMOMILE SPELL FOR WEIGHT LOSS

SPELL INGREDIENTS

- ☆ Blue pen
- ☆ Slim white candle
- ☆ Dried camomile flowers

SPELL WORK

Start this spell on a waning moon. Write your target weight in blue pen on the white candle. Sprinkle camomile flowers around the candle. Before every major meal, light the candle and look at your target-weight number on the candle while chewing one of the flowers. You can renew this spell by adding more camomile flowers as needed.

VERVEINE AND LEMON BALM SPELL TO PROTECT AGAINST INJURY

SPELL INGREDIENTS

- ☆ Verveine
- ☆ Lemon balm
- ☆ Turquoise stone

SPELL WORK

Make a strong infusion with verveine and lemon balm. Drop the turquoise into a cup of the infusion and swirl around gently counter clockwise while saying:

"Bone breaks and illness stay away from me
Get away, leave me be!"

Then swirl clockwise and say:

"I will stay healthy and strong
As surely as the day is long!"

Take the turquoise out and keep it in your pocket as a health talisman. This spell works especially well when being performed before doing risky sports such as skiing or diving.

Luck and anti-negativity spells

NUTMEG AND ALMOND SPELL TO DRAIN AWAY WORRIES

SPELL INGREDIENTS

- ☆ 3 teaspoons grated nutmeg
- ☆ Almond oil

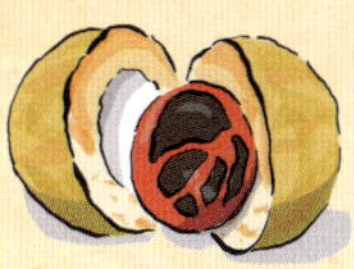

SPELL WORK

Draw a warm bath. Add three teaspoons of grated nutmeg and a little almond oil. Say the following chant three times, submerging yourself fully after each time you say the chant:

"I have had much bad luck
My life is a suck
But goodness and positivity
Happiness too will come to me!"

Pull out the plug and, while still sitting in the bath, watch the water drain down the plug hole. With the water, imagine your worries and bad luck draining away too.

NUTMEG SPELL TO STAMP OUT BAD LUCK

SPELL INGREDIENTS

- ☆ Pen and paper
- ☆ Old shoe
- ☆ Fire
- ☆ 3 whole nutmegs

SPELL WORK

Write all your bad luck and problems on a piece of paper. Put on an old shoe and stomp on the paper three times. Then burn the shoe in a fire and bury the paper, wrapping three whole nutmegs in it. By the time the paper has dissolved into the earth, your problems will have gone away.

THYME SPELL FOR SUCCESS IN TESTS

SPELL INGREDIENTS

- ☆ Dried thyme

SPELL WORK

Before studying for a test or leaving to take an exam, light some dried thyme. Inhale the smoke and visualize yourself opening the envelope with the test results or being given the results by the examiner and feeling very happy. Extinguish the smoldering thyme by holding it under a running tap while saying:

"I'll do well in the test today
Goddess willing, I'll get an A
Earth, Air, Fire, and Sea
As I speak it, so mote it be!"

Spells for Wisdom, Inner Peace, and Meditations

The spells in this section have more of an inner focus, for spiritual and mental self-improvement, than external aims, to gain money, objects, safety, or similar. Green Wicca is just as much about self-improvement, and walking your spiritual path comfortably and securely, than "outward" magic, so the spells in this section are especially important to me.

Wisdom spells are obviously not something you can perform once, and then be a wise crone or sage with all the wisdom of the ages. But they will help you be calm, review situations detachedly, and make the correct decisions not just for you, but for the universe in general. Many witches regularly perform a wisdom spell or a meditation targeted at gaining occult knowledge and wisdom, as it's something you can never have enough of! Other important assets for a witch are self-love and self-confidence. Only when you know and love yourself will you trust your intuition the way a witch should, and have the mental power and spiritual energy to perform the more difficult types of magic that require you to command a lot of energy.

"I died as a mineral and became a plant, I died as plant and rose to animal, I died as animal and I was Man. Why should I fear? When was I less by dying?"

Jalaluddin Rumi (1207–1273)

WORMWOOD, BAY, AND SAGE SPELL FOR WISDOM

SPELL INGREDIENTS

- Charcoal
- Wormwood
- Bay
- Sage

SPELL WORK

Light the charcoal and onto it sprinkle a little dried wormwood, bay, and sage and say:

"Wisdom seek
To illuminate my world bleak
Wisdom I love
And knowledge from above."

Sit quietly for a while, taking in the herbal aroma of the smoke—you can add more herbs to the charcoal as needed. When you feel ready, get up and extinguish the charcoal if still burning. This spell works especially well when performed on a new moon.

SAGE AND BAY SPELL FOR GUIDANCE

SPELL INGREDIENTS

- Sage laves
- Bay leaves
- Purple thread
- An owl statue

SPELL WORK

Tie alternate sage and bay leaves together with the purple thread to make a long necklace that reaches your navel when worn. Place the necklace on the owl statue (which should be on your altar or another place in your home that is important to you) and say:

"Wisdom I seek, to make decisions
Good judgment, without divisions
I want the spirits blessing, not their wrath
I seek wisdom on my spiritual path!"

Leave the necklace on the owl statue. When you feel the need for a bit of extra wisdom or the guidance of knowledge and wisdom spirits, wear the necklace, look at the owl, and meditate on the issue you seek wisdom on.

CARAWAY SEED SPELL FOR INNER PEACE AND HAPPINESS

SPELL INGREDIENTS

- ☆ Red candle
- ☆ Caraway seeds

SPELL WORK

Light the red candle and with your left hand, sprinkle caraway seeds in a clockwise circle around it while saying:

"By this candle flame
I cast away shame
Inner peace I have found
Love and happiness will abound!"

Then take a few caraway seeds with your right hand and place them in your mouth. Feel the seeds in your mouth, then say:

"I eat this caraway seed
For inner strength is my need
Inner peace I have found
Love and happiness will abound!"

Then chew and eat the seeds.

ROSE WATER AND TARRAGON SPELL TO LOVE YOUR BODY

SPELL INGREDIENTS

- ☆ Rose water
- ☆ Tarragon
- ☆ Mirror

SPELL WORK

Mix the rose water and the tarragon. Look at yourself in the mirror. Say something positive about every part of your body and bless it, starting at your feet all the way up to your hair. Do this especially for parts of your body you don't particularly like! Examples might be: "Blessed be my toes, for they are long and can grip things"; "Blessed be my calves, for they are chunky and carry me on long walks"; "Blessed be my breasts, for they are large and get me attention"; "Blessed be my hair, for its color pleases me," and so on. After you have made the positive statement, dab some of the tarragon rose water onto the part. This spell works best when performed naked.

PEPPERCORN AND TARRAGON SPELL FOR CONFIDENCE

SPELL INGREDIENTS

- ☆ Tarragon
- ☆ Red peppercorns

SPELL WORK

Hold some tarragon in one hand and some red peppercorns in the other. Stand with your feet hip-width apart and your hands at your side, a few inches away from your body. Feel warmth rising from Mother Earth to fill you with Her love and confidence in you. Feel warmth flowing down from Father Sky to fill you with His strength and confidence in you. Sprinkle the peppercorns and tarragon on your head, forming a shield around you.

A SPELL TO MAKE BLESSING OIL

SPELL INGREDIENTS

- ☆ Marjoram
- ☆ Black peppercorns
- ☆ Cumin seeds
- ☆ Sunflower oil

SPELL WORK

Add the marjoram, black peppercorns, and cumin to the sunflower oil. Swirl with your right little finger while saying nine times:

"Cleanse and consecrate
Wonderful magic I'll create!"

Then swirl with your left little finger while saying:

"Blessed be
This oil to me."

You now have a blessing oil with which to consecrate your magical tools, to use on yourself before a ritual or for blessing newly purchased objects. You can make this oil ahead of time and keep it in a dark glass bottle.

PARSLEY SPELL FOR CONTACT WITH THOSE WHO HAVE PASSED ON

SPELL INGREDIENTS

- ☆ Black candle
- ☆ Photo of, or something belonging to, the deceased
- ☆ Parsley
- ☆ Purple bag (ideally silk)

SPELL WORK

Light the candle and slow your breathing. Place the photo in front of the candle flame and look "through" it, as if still looking at the flame. Say:

"Through the veil you fell
But through this spell
I ask to contact thee
If for the good of all it be."

Blow out the candle gently and watch the smoke waft away; imagine this smoke carrying your request to the deceased. Put the candle stub, photo, and parsley into the purple bag then place it under your pillow and go to sleep. You should dream of the deceased that night but if not, or if you cannot remember the dream, go for a walk first thing in the morning (before having anything to eat or drink) with the bag held in your left hand, and if the deceased wishes contact, Mother Nature may be your go-between.

HERBAL SPELL TO HELP MEDITATION

SPELL INGREDIENTS

- ☆ Sage
- ☆ Juniper
- ☆ Rue
- ☆ Cumin
- ☆ An open fire (fireplace, BBQ, or even a fire in a large fireproof cauldron)

SPELL WORK

Mix the herbal ingredients in your left hand. Throw into the open fire just before doing a meditation. Sage cleanses the mind, juniper will bring psychic awareness, rue, occult knowledge, and cumin psychic protection, so you can get the most out of your meditation and be safe from malevolent entities.

Chapter 7

Magical Herbs: Kitchen Witchery

When herbs have been grown and stored with care, and with magical intent, they will always have some magical energy in them—and of course that is what this book is all about.

This chapter is concerned with a more gentle type of magic: not spells and rituals, nor invocation of deities or meditations. Instead, it is about kitchen witchery—using magical herbs to add an extra dimension to your food and drink, as well as in alternative medicines.

The recipes and suggestions in this chapter are ideal to share with non-Wiccan friends and family, as you do not need to be an experienced witch, or a Wiccan by religion, to follow any of the suggestions here.

Also included in this chapter are herbal recipes for beauty, plus other ways to subtly add magical energy to your home, such as with an attractive, scented wall pomander.

Making Magical Potions

In Chapter 3, page 42, I explain how to store herbs safely without losing their magical energy or taste (such as drying, keeping them in oil, and pressing). Here, I list some simple, generic recipes for making magical incense as well as infusions, ointments, and syrups suitable for medicine and kitchen witchery, which can be used with any herb.

How to make incense

It is easy to make loose incense, which you can burn over a piece of charcoal or toss into a small fire in a cauldron or in your fireplace. Simply ensure your herbs are dried thoroughly, then crush them finely (it is best to use a mortar and pestle for this) and add pinches to the smoldering charcoal as you go along.

I love using my own loose incense to cleanse a room before a coven ritual, or before I meditate! It gives some extra, personal energy to the task. I add sandalwood to most of my incenses as it is protective and promotes spiritual awareness—it also makes loose incense burn for longer. Homemade loose incense will usually last for one year or more.

Incense sticks are easier to use than loose incense. They are less messy, as you don't need to add herbs as they burn, but making your own incense sticks is quite difficult and takes time. I haven't yet been able to make a herbal mixture that dries evenly and doesn't crumble off the stick!

If you do want to personalize ready-made incense sticks, try those scented with sandalwood (for protection) or geranium (to clear negativity), then dip them into an essential oil. This will help with whatever magic you want to do, or the energy you want to promote in your home or office. Don't let an incense stick stand in the essential oil, as it will dissolve; just dip it quickly or dab some essential oil onto the stick, then let it dry before use. This is especially useful if you want to dip the incense sticks in different oils to evoke different magical qualities as it burns, or reuse the stick again at a later date..

How to make infusions and syrups

Infusions and syrups are basically concentrated herbal liquids. They are good for concentrating the energy of a magical herb or herbal mixture, and also tend to last longer than herbal teas or fresh herbs. Syrups and infusions are a good way to preserve herbs when they are not in season, or whenever you simply do not have them available (syrups are a great way to swap herbs, too!). Infusions will last for up two weeks or so; syrups can last for around nine months, provided you keep them in the fridge.

Infusions can be particularly useful if you wish to concentrate a herb's smell, as well as when mixing different herbs, especially when trying to mask the bitterness or taste of a certain herb. For example, some people do not like the taste of camomile, so one solution would be to make a mixed infusion of camomile with peppermint.

INFUSIONS

When making an infusion, never boil the water the way you might for tea, but just bring it to near-boiling point. Slowly pour the hot water over the magical herbs. Stir clockwise, letting them infuse for ten minutes or, if you can, wait until the water is room temperature before bottling or using it. How much water to use with your herbs depends on how strong you want your infusion to be and whether you are using fresh or dried herbs (fresh herbs usually need more water, as they are less potent and fragrant than dried herbs). As a guideline, I would suggest about 17 fl oz (0.5 liters) of water for every 4 oz (100 g) of fresh herb.

SYRUPS

A syrup goes one step further than an infusion—adding sugar makes the infusion more pleasant to taste and helps preserve it. The easiest way to make a syrup is to add about 17 fl oz (0.5 liters) of herbal infusion to about 1 lb (0.5 kg) of sugar. Put into a saucepan and simmer and stir until the sugar is completely dissolved before bottling your syrup. Keep it in the fridge if possible.

How to make an ointment

Ointments allow you to keep magical herbs for longer, but tend to be used more commonly in alternative medicine rather than in the spells and rituals of magic. The exception to this is blessing ointments, which are used when welcoming new coven members, or in health spells that combine alternative medicine and magic.

To make an ointment, heat a pure, plain fat such as lard or petroleum jelly in a bain marie (a bowl placed in hot water). When the fat begins to melt into liquid, stir in your essential oils or crushed fresh herbs—the amount depends purely on personal taste—and keep this semi-fluid for an hour or so, stirring often before pouring it into small jars or tins. It's best to use sterilized jars, or at least wash them in a hot dishwasher first. Let the mixture cool and solidify before putting on lids; if you are using glass or other see-through containers, store them in a dark place. The ointment will last for around nine months. However, if you use inferior fat the ointment can go stale—you will know by the smell.

SPELL

If you are trying to study for an exam, use a cinnamon incense stick. Dip the tip into geranium oil to clear your head at the beginning of your study, and dab thyme oil onto the rest of the stick to help with concentration and success. Light the incense, and extinguish at the end of your study session.

Food and Drink

Just because you use a magical herb in a food or drink, it doesn't mean you must perform a spell or chant over it—though you certainly can, and it will help with any other spell or ritual you'll perform after eating. But using magical herbs will make your life magical when you do not have time to get changed into a robe and meditate, or attend a coven ritual. Be mindful of all ingredients you use in your recipes, not just the magical herb—everything has an energy!

SALTED HERBS

INGREDIENTS

- ☆ 2 OZ (50 G) CHOPPED CHIVES
- ☆ 2 OZ (50 G) CHOPPED PARSLEY
- ☆ 2 OZ (50 G) CHOPPED CARROTS
- ☆ 2 OZ (50 G) CHOPPED FENNEL
- ☆ 2 OZ (50 G) CHOPPED CELERY
- ☆ 2 OZ (50 G) CHOPPED ONION
- ☆ 4 OZ (100 G) COARSE SALT
- ☆ 4 CRUSHED GARLIC CLOVES (OPTIONAL)

PREPARATION

Mix together all the herbs and vegetables. Layer 1 in (2.5 cm) of the mixture at the bottom of a large glass jar or small crock pot. Sprinkle with a layer of salt. Repeat with further layers until all the vegetable herb mixture is used, and finish off with a layer of salt. Cover and keep in the fridge for at least a week (two to three weeks is better), draining off any liquid that may accumulate every few days. Great in casseroles, on pasta, and in anything else you would want to add salt to give it flavor.

Salted herbs have a range of magical qualities, but mainly they will make you confident (due to the fennel and chives) and, if you've just eaten them at dinner, will help you discern the truth of statements spoken around the dinner table (due to the parsley and celery). The salted carrot and parsley encourage virility and fertility, so are great to eat if you are trying to conceive! You can experiment with different herbs and vegetables to get different magical and flavor results.

QUICK GINGERBREAD

INGREDIENTS

- ☆ 2 OZ (50 G) HONEY
- ☆ 1 TEASPOON FINELY CHOPPED GINGER OR ¼ TEASPOON GINGER POWDER
- ☆ 1/8 TEASPOON GROUND CLOVES
- ☆ 1/8 TEASPOON GROUND CINNAMON
- ☆ 1/8 TEASPOON GROUND ALLSPICE
- ☆ 1/8 TEASPOON GROUND STAR ANISE
- ☆ 1 TABLESPOON ANISE SEEDS
- ☆ 4 OZ (100 G) BREADCRUMBS

PREPARATION

Warm the honey until gently simmering, then slowly add all the spices except the anise seeds. Add the dry breadcrumbs and mix well. Continue simmering gently for 15 to 20 minutes. The consistency should be one of very thick molasses; you may need to add a little more honey or breadcrumbs to achieve the correct consistency. Pour onto waxed paper and sprinkle the anise seeds on top, pressing them into the gingerbread gently so they stick. Let the gingerbread cool a little and then cut into squares or use cookie cutters to get all kinds of fun shapes. Place in the fridge or outside in winter for a couple of hours to let it cool and set. Serve at room temperature—great with ice cream too! In German, gingerbread is called lebkuchen (life cake), because the ingredients magically enhance and protect your life, such as removing negativity and curses (through the cloves and star anise); bringing luck (via the allspice and anise), and providing success (via the cinnamon).

To add an extra flavor and magical dimension to your pastry, add some thyme to the dough, which will help keep you healthy and successful in your work. This works especially well in pie crusts and filo pastry for sweet treats.

HERBAL ICE BOWL

INGREDIENTS

- ☆ Lavender flowers
- ☆ Dandelion leaves
- ☆ Camomile flowers
- ☆ Star anise
- ☆ Elderflowers

An ice bowl can make a wonderful, magical centerpiece when you have guests for dinner or are hosting a party. You can use it as a sculpture, or fill it with punch, iced soup, fruit salad, or ice-cream, and it is easier to make than you may think! You can use any pretty herbs and flowers you like, but used in this recipe are the ones I recommend.

PREPARATION

Take two bowls, one larger than the other. When the smaller bowl is placed in the large bowl, there should be a gap of $3/4$–$1\,1/2$ in (2 cm–$3\,3/4$ cm) between the outside edges of the two bowls.

Fill the larger bowl with 2 in (5 cm) of water and semi-freeze. Remove the large bowl from the refrigerator and place the smaller bowl inside, making sure it sits in the center (a weight inside the smaller bowl is a good idea).

Fill 2 in (5 cm) of the space between the bowls with water and add some of the herbal leaves and flowers. Place the bowls back in the freezer for 15 minutes to let the water semi-freeze, then repeat until you have reached the top (be careful not to let each layer freeze completely, as that may stop the layers from holding together).

Place in the freezer until the water is frozen solid, then remove the ice bowl from the two bowls you used by gently wiping the inside of the smaller bowl with a warm cloth and doing the same to the outside of the larger bowl. Remove the small bowl first, and then lift the ice bowl from the large bowl.

Make sure you stand the ice bowl on a large dinner plate to catch the drips as it slowly melts.

QUICK HERBAL JELLOS

INGREDIENTS

- ☆ 2 TABLESPOONS SUGAR
- ☆ 7 FL OZ (ABOUT 0.25 LITERS) GRAPE JUICE
- ☆ 4 SPRIGS BERGAMOT
- ☆ 1 TABLESPOON POWDERED GELATINE OR EQUIVALENT VEGETARIAN GELATINE (SUCH AS PECTIN OR ALGAE), DISSOLVED IN A LITTLE WATER
- ☆ 10 SEEDLESS GREEN GRAPES

PREPARATION

Place the sugar (a magical symbol of luck and luxury), grape juice (for prosperity), and bergamot sprigs (again, for luck) into a small pan and bring to a boil. Let the mixture cool a bit, then remove the bergamot. Add the dissolved gelatine and stir gently until mixed completely. Place half of the mixture into a bowl, allow to cool until semi-set, then add the grapes. Pour over the rest of the mixture and let it set in the fridge. Alternatively, you can make individual jellos in cups or champagne glasses, and decorate each with a sprig of bergamot.

HERB CHEESE

INGREDIENTS

- ☆ 17 FL OZ (0.5 LITERS) PLAIN LIVE YOGURT
- ☆ 1/2 TEASPOON SALT
- ☆ 1 TABLESPOON CHOPPED TARRAGON
- ☆ 1 TABLESPOON CHOPPED CHIVES
- ☆ 1 TABLESPOON CHOPPED PARSLEY
- ☆ BLACK PEPPER, TO TASTE
- ☆ CHEESECLOTH

PREPARATION

Place the cheesecloth in a sieve and place over a large bowl. Mix the yogurt and salt and pour the mixture gently into the sieve. Place the sieve and bowl into the fridge for a day or two until the yogurt is firm and the whey liquid has drained into the bowl. Transfer the now-firm yoghurt into a bowl and mix gently with the herbs and pepper. Your homemade cheese is now ready for crackers! Alternatively, you can leave the parsley out of the herb mixture and make small cheese balls, then roll them in the chopped parsley for decoration. I'd recommend always using parsley for its cleansing effect, which is great after meals and magical rituals, and using pepper for protection, but you can vary the other herbs depending on your personal taste and magical intention.

CINNAMON HARD CANDY

INGREDIENTS

- 2 oz (50 g) sugar
- 3½ fl oz (100 ml) maple syrup
- 1 teaspoon ground cinnamon
- Pinch of chili, if desired
- Red food coloring, if desired
- Powdered sugar

PREPARATION

Mix the sugar, maple syrup, and 3½ fl oz (100 ml) water in a pan and heat to boiling, stirring constantly, until the mixture thickens considerably (this will happen quickly) and the sugar cracks when a drop is placed into cold water (be careful, as boiling sugar is very, very hot). Remove from the heat and add the cinnamon, chili, and food coloring, if desired. Pour onto a baking tray that has been thickly coated with powdered sugar, and pour some powdered sugar on top. Start cutting into small squares immediately, starting at the outside, as this mixture will set very quickly.

Because magically cinnamon symbolizes love and lust, especially when combined with chili, this is a great candy to share with that special loved one, or to make for Valentine's Day.

HERB EASTER EGG

INGREDIENTS

- Small feverfew leaves
- Wild garlic flowers
- Parsley leaves
- Star anise
- Red clover leaves
- White eggs
- Red or brown onions
- Old pantyhose/tights

PREPARATION

Place some of the herbal leaves and flowers on a white egg. Place the egg gently in the foot of the pantyhose (tights) and tie off, so the herbs are kept in place. Repeat with several eggs. Bring the water to boil in a pan and add the skin of the red or brown onion (depending on whether you want red or brown eggs). Slowly place the eggs-in-tights into the boiling water and boil until they become hard-boiled eggs (usually up to 4 minutes). Remove, allow to cool, cut open the pantyhose, and take off the herbs; you will have hard-boiled eggs that are brown or red with lovely herbal leaves and flowers standing out in white as decorations; the eggs will also have a faint herbal taste to them. The herbs I suggest here are only to get you started—you can use any small herbal leaf or flat flower. Not just for Easter, these will look beautiful on any Sunday brunch table, or can be used on the magical altar to represent almost any magical intent.

LAVENDER LEMONADE SYRUP

INGREDIENTS

- ☆ 10 RED CLOVER FLOWERS
- ☆ 4 OZ (100 G) LAVENDER
- ☆ 4 OZ 1(00 G) SUGAR
- ☆ 3 1/3 FL OZ (100 ML) LEMON JUICE
- ☆ ICE-CUBE TRAY

PREPARATION

Place one red clover flower in each individual ice-cube tray, then fill with water and freeze. Put all the ingredients except for the lemon juice in a pan with 10 fl oz(0.3 liters) water and bring to the boil. As soon as it is boiling, remove from the heat and cool in the fridge overnight; you now have a pale pink liquid. Just before serving, add the lemon juice and dilute with more water until desired strength is reached. Decorate with the red clover ice cubes.

GRIPE WATER

INGREDIENTS

- ☆ 1 TEASPOON DILL SEEDS
- ☆ 1 TEASPOON CRUSHED FENNEL SEEDS
- ☆ JUST UNDER 1 OZ (20 G) BROWN SUGAR (OPTIONAL)

PREPARATION

Boil 18 fl oz (0.5 liters) water and pour over the dill and fennel seeds. Let this infuse for 20 minutes. Strain out the seeds. Add brown sugar if desired, and make sure it dissolves completely.

The mixture, which is great for relieving trapped wind, can be stored in the fridge for a couple of days and should be drunk at room temperature.

ELDERBERRY SYRUP

INGREDIENTS

- ☆ 2 LEMONS
- ☆ 2 LB (1 KILO) ELDERBERRIES
- ☆ 2 OZ (50 G) JASMINE FLOWERS
- ☆ 2 OZ (50 G) CITRONELLA LEAVES
- ☆ 20 OZ (50 G) SUGAR

PREPARATION

Gently grate the rind off the top of the lemons, then juice them. Mix the elderberries, 18 fl oz (0.5 liters) water, lemon juice, and rind in a pan and bring to the boil. Let it cool a bit, then add the jasmine flowers, citronella leaves, and sugar. Bring to the boil again while gently stirring, and allow to boil for five minutes. Strain through a sieve or cheesecloth, decant into warm flasks or bottles, and keep them somewhere dry and dark; if opened, keep in the fridge. Add to mineral water to taste; I recommend a ratio of about ¼ syrup to ¾ water. The elderberry's health and protection qualities combined with citronella's happiness, jasmine's love, and lemon's friendship power make this a truly magical drink.

FLOWER TEA

INGREDIENTS

EQUAL PARTS OF

- ☆ Red clover
- ☆ Lemon balm
- ☆ Peppermint
- ☆ Rose petals
- ☆ Cornflower
- ☆ Marigold
- ☆ Lime tree blossom
- ☆ Honey, to taste

A pretty tea, great for summer parties, which also promotes health. You can also try this mixture to bring some summer into dreary winter days!

PREPARATION

Mix together all the ingredients, then pour boiling water over them. It's up to you how strong to make the infusion, but I personally use a small handful of each herb to a quart (about a liter) of water. Allow to infuse for a minimum of five minutes. You can strain out the herbs, although I'd recommend not doing this at all as they do look pretty in the infusion. Add honey to taste.

COUGH TEAS

INGREDIENTS

(ALL DRIED)

- ☆ 2 OZ (50 G) SAGE
- ☆ 2 OZ (50 G) MARJORAM
- ☆ 10 STAR ANISE
- ☆ 2 OZ (50 G) COLTSFOOT

OR

- ☆ 2 OZ (50 G) THYME
- ☆ 2 OZ (50 G) VERBENA
- ☆ 2 OZ (50 G) FENNEL
- ☆ 2 OZ (50 G) MULLEIN FLOWERS
- ☆ HONEY OR MOLASSES, TO TASTE

Two teas to combat colds and coughs.

PREPARATION

Mix together all the ingredients. Use three pinches of the mixture for a large cup of tea, add boiling water, and let it steep for five to ten minutes. You can strain out the herbs or keep them in the tea for tea-leaf reading after you finished drinking. Sweeten with honey or molasses if desired.

SOOTHING STOMACH TEA

INGREDIENTS

(DRIED HERBS)

- ☆ 2 OZ (50 G) PEPPERMINT
- ☆ 2 OZ (50 G) CAMOMILE
- ☆ 3/4 OZ (20 G) WORMWOOD
- ☆ PINCH CARAWAY SEEDS

The perfect tea to settle a bloated, painful stomach.

PREPARATION

Mix all the ingredients together. Use about three pinches to make a large cup of tea; infuse in boiling water and strain off the herbs. It is best not to use sweetener to ensure this tea can work its best.

SLEEP TEA

INGREDIENTS

(DRIED HERBS)

- ☆ 2 OZ (50 G) ELDER FLOWERS
- ☆ 2 OZ (50 G) LAVENDER
- ☆ 2 OZ (50 G) HAWTHORN FLOWERS
- ☆ 2 OZ (50 G) HOPS FLOWERS
- ☆ 2 OZ (50 G) VALERIAN LEAVES
- ☆ 2 OZ (50 G) BASIL LEAVES

This tea will help you go to sleep after a stressful day or when suffering from insomnia.

PREPARATION

Mix everything together. Use about three pinches to make a large cup of tea; infuse in boiling water and strain off the herbs. Drink about 45 minutes prior to bedtime.

FEVER TEA

INGREDIENTS

(DRIED HERBS)

- ☆ 3/4 OZ (20 G) THYME FLOWERS
- ☆ 3/4 OZ (20 G) HOLLY LEAVES
- ☆ 3/4 OZ (20 G) ELDER FLOWERS
- ☆ 3/4 OZ (20 G) LIME FLOWERS
- ☆ 3/4 OZ (20 G) 20 G MEADOWSWEET
- ☆ HONEY OR MOLASSES, TO TASTE

This tea helps break a fever, ease rheumatism, and strengthen the constitution after an illness.

PREPARATION

Mix together all the ingredients. Use about three pinches to make a large cup of tea; infuse in boiling water and strain off the herbs. Sweeten with honey or molasses if desired.

Beauty

Magical beauty recipes will not only make you more beautiful because their ingredients make your skin more healthy or your hair more shiny, but they also work on two other, possibly more important levels: the herbs in these beauty tips add their magical energy to enchant you and those around you to see you as more beautiful, and they will raise your self-confidence and inner strength.

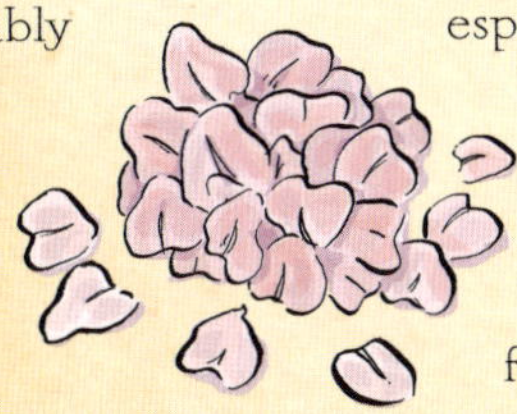

You will end up beautiful inside and out, magically and physically. With beauty herbs, you always need to ensure they are not toxic, especially when using concentrated essential oils. Also keep in mind that if you are pregnant or nursing, some herbs may not be recommended to use during that time, so always consult a healthcare professional for advice.

MAGICAL NAIL POLISH

Add five drops of an appropriate essential oil to your favorite nail polish, or choose a nail-polish color appropriate to your magical intent. For example:

- ☆ Add five drops of rose essential oil to red nail polish on a waxing moon to see your nails, and your love life, grow.
- ☆ Add five drops of fennel essential oil to clear nail polish on a full moon to gain inner strength and believe in yourself.
- ☆ Add five drops of basil essential oil to gold nail polish on a waxing moon to improve your finances.

The quantities above assume you have a full bottle of nail polish. If you are using less than a full bottle, add proportionately less essential oil or you could over-dilute the nail polish, and it won't coat your nails or dry properly.

BATH SPRINKLE

INGREDIENTS

- ☆ 10 rose petals
- ☆ 5 sprigs lavender
- ☆ Cheesecloth (use yellow for friendship, pink for love, or white for peace)

PREPARATION

Crush the rose petals and lavender a little, then place in the middle of the cheesecloth and tie the ends together to make a ball. Drop into a warm running bath.

ROSE RENEWAL SPRAY

INGREDIENTS

- 2 TABLESPOONS CRUSHED ROSE PETALS
- 2 TABLESPOONS ROSEMARY
- 5 EUCALYPTUS LEAVES
- 1 TABLESPOON VITAMIN C (YOU CAN GET PURE VITAMIN C—ALSO CALLED ASCORBIC ACID—IN PHARMACIES OR HEALTH-FOOD STORES, BUT IF YOU CANNOT OBTAIN IT, USE A CRUSHED VITAMIN C TABLET).

PREPARATION

Bring 10 fl oz (0.3 liters) water to a gentle simmer, then add the rose petals, rosemary, and eucalyptus. Do not boil! Leave simmering for 15 minutes. Cool to room temperature, then strain out the herbs and add the vitamin C. Pour into a dark bottle and use as a make-up remover (to use as eye make-up remover, the mixture needs to be more diluted more—use double the quantity of water); or place in a spray bottle and use to freshen your face in the morning or after being in a stuffy room. It will keep for a couple of weeks if refrigerated.

NOURISHING LIP GLOSS

INGREDIENTS

- 2 OZ (50 G) BEESWAX
- 2 OZ (50 G) CASTOR OIL
- BEET JUICE
- 2 DROPS OF ANY EDIBLE ESSENTIAL OIL IF DESIRED, SUCH AS ALLSPICE, CINNAMON, CITRONELLA, SAGE, LAVENDER, PEPPERMINT, BASIL, CLOVE, NUTMEG, ROSEMARY, OR JASMINE
- CATNIP LEAVES

PREPARATION

Melt the beeswax and add the caster oil. Add beet juice (how much will depend on how red you want your lip gloss to be—the more beet you add, the deeper the color). Then add the drops of essential oil to give the lip gloss flavor, and to add an extra magical dimension.

Line a small jar with catnip leaves and pour in the mixture. Leave to cool, and it's ready to use!

BEAUTIFYING BLESSING OIL

INGREDIENTS

- ☆ 10 DROPS CITRONELLA OIL
- ☆ 10 DROPS GERANIUM OIL
- ☆ 20 DROPS ORANGE OIL
- ☆ 20 CUMIN SEEDS
- ☆ 3 1/3 FL OZ (100 ML) ALMOND OIL

PREPARATION

Combine the ingredients by adding the essential oils and cumin seeds slowly into the almond oil one by one. Use as a massage oil, on your hands before going out to a party or as a blessing oil on things you use to beautify yourself, such as hair brushes, or nail files.

STRENGTHENING HAIR RINSE

INGREDIENTS

- ☆ 5 SPRIGS ROSEMARY
- ☆ HANDFUL OF CAMOMILE FLOWERS
- ☆ 3 1/3 FL OZ (100 ML) LEMON JUICE

PREPARATION

Place the rosemary and camomile in a bowl. Add 10 fl oz (0.3 liters) freshly boiled water and leave to infuse until the water reaches room temperature. Strain the herbs out and add the lemon juice, then place the liquid in a bottle. Use as a final rinse after shampooing and conditioning your hair.

Other Ways to Use Herbs

There is really no end to the way magical herbs can be used outside of magic. Just go with your intuition and creativity! Here are some ideas how I have used herbs in unusual ways to decorate my home and myself and bring a little gentle magic into my life. I hope these will serve to get you started, and that you will keep experimenting after trying these out!

QUICK POMANDER

INGREDIENTS

- 10 cloves
- Lemon or orange
- Rosemary sprigs, thistles, or juniper branches if desired
- Gold ribbon

PREPARATION

A quick way to add magic to your home and make it smell nice is to spike a lemon or orange with cloves. You can add other woody herbs such as rosemary sprigs, thistles, or juniper branches—any you can push directly into the lemon or orange—to add to the magic of your pomander. Tie with the gold ribbon and place on a dresser or bookshelf, or hang from a curtain rod.

WALL POMANDER

INGREDIENTS

- Long, flowering lavender sprigs (for relaxation, peace, friendship, happiness)
- Long basil sprigs (money, prosperity, fortune-telling, inner strength)
- Flowering oregano sprigs (health, happiness)
- Twine
- Ribbon

PREPARATION

Tie five to ten sprigs of each individual herb together with twine so they reach a finger's-width thickness. Do this several times, then tie the bunches together at one end with a pretty ribbon; you'll end up with lavender, basil, and oregano "cords" of about a meter (just over a yard) each. Braid the three cords together as you would hair to combine their magical intent and bring peace from the lavender, prosperity from the basil, and health and happiness from the oregano into your home. If desired, you can use the ribbon to braid with in a four-cord braid, and use a magical color such as blue for health, green for prosperity, or pink for romantic love—whatever is needed most in your home. Tie off the end with ribbon again, and hang on a wall for a pleasant-smelling wall decoration.

HERBAL FLOWER CENTERPIECE

INGREDIENTS

- 3 VERBENA STALKS
- 3 LAVENDER SPRIGS
- 3 ROSEMARY SPRIGS
- 3 BASIL SPRIGS
- 3 SAGE SPRIGS
- 3 CAMOMILE STALKS
- WHITE PAPER OR LACE
- RIBBON

This centerpiece is lovely on any table and makes the perfect gift. It not only smells and looks nice, but it's also useful! You can use fresh or dried herbs.

PREPARATION

Gather the herbs together into a bouquet so they alternate, then tie together with some ribbon. Wrap the lace around it to make a collar; if you cannot find lace, you can make a stencil with white paper and use that. Tie off with more ribbon and you are done!

HERBAL INSECT REPELLANT

INGREDIENTS

- 5 CITRONELLA LEAVES
- 5 BASIL LEAVES
- 5 MINT LEAVES
- 5 CLOVES
- ORGANZA SQUARE (PREFERABLY BLUE FOR HEALTH OR SILVER FOR THE BLESSING OF THE MOON GODDESS IN KEEPING NIGHT-TIME INSECTS AWAY, BUT ANY COLOR WILL DO)
- RIBBON

PREPARATION

Place the herbs in the middle of the organza square. Bring up the corners and tie off with the ribbon to make a little round parcel. Place in windows, on outdoors tables, or in closets. Works especially well to ward off mosquitoes in summer when you have the windows open at night.

FLEA-REPELLANT PET PILLOW

INGREDIENTS

- ☆ 2 OZ (50 G) DRIED PENNYROYAL
- ☆ 3/4 OZ (20 G) DRIED THYME
- ☆ 3/4 OZ (20 G) DRIED WORMWOOD
- ☆ 3/4 OZ (20 G) DRIED CATNIP

PREPARATION

Mix together all the ingredients. If your dog or cat has a special bed, you can open a seam and sprinkle the herbs inside to create a flea-repellant pet bed. If you like to cover your pet with a fleece or they like to lay on one, rub some of the herbal mixture into the fleece.

SLEEP POSEY

INGREDIENTS

- ☆ 10 SPRIGS LAVENDER
- ☆ 10 SPRIGS ROSEMARY
- ☆ BLUE RIBBON

PREPARATION

Gather the lavender and rosemary in a bunch and tie with the blue ribbon (for healing, wisdom, and calm). Hang this from a bedpost or leave on your bedside table.

HERBAL HAT

INGREDIENTS

- ☆ Small bunch of parsley, feverfew, red clover, camphor, and thistle
- ☆ Straw hat
- ☆ Thin ribbon

PREPARATION

For a magical hat to wear to a summer picnic or outdoor event, such as a wedding or at the races, gather the fresh herbs listed here (or any other herbs which suit the outfit you plan on wearing and your magical intent) the morning of the event. Gather the herbs into small mixed bunches—not all bunches need to include the same herbs, but they should all be roughly the same size. Place the bunches one after the other at the base of the rim of your hat and tie to the hat with thin ribbon to create a herbal circle around the hat.

HERBAL PLANT SPRAY

INGREDIENTS

- ☆ 3/4 oz (20 g) chili
- ☆ 10 red peppercorns
- ☆ 3 whole wild garlic (or 5 garlic cloves if you cannot find wild)
- ☆ 3 citronella leaves
- ☆ 3/4 fl oz (20 g) mild fluid soap (preferably odorless)
- ☆ Spray bottle

To keep your magical herbs, vegetables, and fruits free from insects and snails, use this spray on them.

PREPARATION

Add 3 3/4 fl oz (100 ml) water and the herbs to a blender and blend until completely smooth. Pour into a spray bottle. Add soap and fill up with water. Spray your garden when there is no direct sunlight.

Chapter 8

How to Write your own Magical Spells

Chapter 6 gave you a wide selection of spells from my personal Book of Shadows; all those spells have been tested, and work. Some are a few hundred years old, or based on old spell books; others I got from my Wiccan teachers, but most I have written myself for my own use, coven members, and readers of my published work in magazines and books. So why am I encouraging you to write your own spells, when I could fill a whole other book with spells and sell it to you instead? Simple: I want you to have the most powerful, most successful spells available.

While my spells have worked for me and for those I know, they may not work for you, which is why personalizing your spells can be just the solution you need. There are many reasons for this: because the energies are different where you live, or because the spell technique doesn't suit you—for example, I may have provided a candle spell for a particular issue when you prefer to do witch-bottle or knot spells.

Another reason why a spell might not work could be because a herb I suggest is unavailable where you live, or because I feel that blue is the best color for spiritual healing, but you have found that green works better for you... and so on.

Writing your own spells enables you to customize the spell or ritual so it fits your situation, magical ability, and preferences perfectly, and you can add your own energy not just during the spell-work itself, but also while writing the spell.

Spell-writing to Empower your Personal Magic

When writing your own spells, first you need to consider if you really need a spell. Sometimes performing magic seems the easy option, compared to working hard and looking into the non-magical way of getting the result you want. But while it may be tempting to choose the time-saving magic spell over a night spent studying, magic actually takes a lot of time to prepare properly, including spiritual and mental energy.

Then you need to decide what kind of spell you want to perform. Are you sick and need healing? Are you drowning in debt? Does your relationship need strengthening? Keep in mind that writing, preparing, and performing strong magic takes time and energy, and unless you are an experienced witch, you are unlikely to be able to perform more than one successful spell every few days (depending on the magnitude or energy requirement of the spell). Once you decide on the kind of spell, you need to decide on the exact intent. If you decide to work on your debt problem magically, do you want to perform magic to lessen the debt (a very specific spell) or a spell for a pay rise at work (a little less specific), or just a general spell to draw money to you?

Even if you are ready to write your own spells, have a look at my list of spells in the previous chapter. The introduction to each subtopic will provide you with some guidelines on how to write a spell for that particular intent, and tips on what to look out for.

Traditions are there for a reason—because they are known to work, sometimes over centuries. But don't be afraid to be non-traditional if it works for you: pink is the traditional color for romantic love, but if you have always associated pale green with love because your first love gave you a pale green scarf, then use that color in your love magic instead.

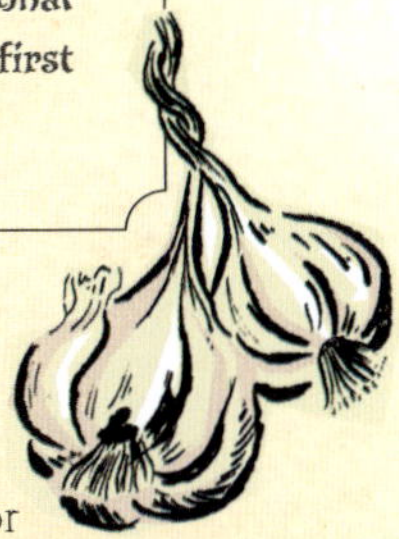

Spell ingredients

Your next step is to decide on the ingredients for your herbal spell. The "52 Major Magical Herbs" chapter (see page 48) will come in useful here! For ease of reference, I have provided some magical correspondence tables at the end of this chapter (see page 154), so you can easily look up which colors go with which herbs, what days of the week are best for what types of magic, and so on. Depending on which spell ingredients you need, it may take you a while to gather them. For example, if your spell requires a whole mandrake root, don't be tempted to take shortcuts; the better quality your spell ingredients, the more energy they'll have and the better the chances of success for your spell.

While it is nice to have a cupboard full of crystals, dried herbs, magical tools, and all kinds of colored candles (and most witches, after a few years of practicing, will acquire these one by one), this is not necessary. You can be creative and make your own, and in the process make your magic stronger by putting more of your own time and energy into it. For example, if the spell you wish to perform calls for the casting of a magical circle with a wand, you could cast a simple circle with your hands instead, find a nice branch from an oak tree to serve as an instant wand, or make your own by tying together some twigs of herbs with a suitably colored thread.

Of course, you might also take the opposite route, especially if you have limited access to spell ingredients, witchy shops, or online supply stores: see what you have around and then base your spell on that. This can be good training for writing spells, as it forces you to really think about what spells you can perform with what is available to you, and will hone your creativity and resourcefulness.

Once you have decided on your spell ingredients and have got them in the house, gather your ingredients so you have them all in one place and don't need to break your concentration by leaving your altar to get a herb from the kitchen, or realizing halfway through your magical spell work that you in fact don't have the green thread needed for the spell.

If you like one of the spells in the earlier chapter, but don't have the herb suggested, look up the "52 Major Magical Herbs" chapter (see page 48) and use another herb with similar magical properties. For example, in a money spell that uses pennyroyal, use the easily obtainable basil instead, or if you have a clump of nettles in your garden, use that for any healing spells.

If you don't feel confident enough to write your own spell from scratch, or want to gain some experience first, try customizing one of my spells—or any spell from a book, or a spell found on the internet. You could add a chant to a spell without an existing vocal element, or change the color of gemstone used in the spell.

Deciding when the spell should be performed

Magic is powerful, and a spell will always have some energy, no matter when it is being performed. But exactly because magic is about energy, a spell will work better when you choose an auspicious time. There is no hard and fast rule about this: for example, if you are writing a love spell, you might decide that Friday (day of love Goddess Venus) is the best day to perform the spell, as that would be the traditional time to work love magic. But if you are trying to attract a man, you might choose Sunday instead, the day of the Sun God and great for dealing with male energies.

A Spell for Good Health

INGREDIENTS

- ☆ 8 Feverfew flowers
- ☆ Eucalyptus oil

A spell to encourage good health and harmony.

PREPARATION

Take the feverfew flowers and dip them in eycaluptus oil. Lay down on the floor, then place one flower each on your right and left foot, right and left knee, pelvic area, each breast, and forehead. Say:

"Gods and Goddesses of Healing, I call on you
Bring with you your magic too
For I am unhealthy and wish not to be
Grant me your power to live in health and harmony
So mote it be!"

Close your eyes and imagine the oil seeping into you, flushing away any sickness. Then imagine the flowers healing you of any illness or discomfort you have.

Moon Magic for Casting Spells

The tables of magical correspondences at the end of this chapter are an easy guide to help you decide on when your spell will work best, but before you get to that section I want to talk some more about the importance of moon phases in magical timing, as it is of primary importance. The moon has four primary phases: new, waxing, full, and waning (see also page 31). There are several secondary phases, such as the quarter moons and the dark moon, for example, but for magic, usually only the four primary moon phases are important. That being said, if you have written a spell and feel it is perfect, but it just doesn't quite work, maybe you could perform it toward the end of the waxing moon rather than the beginning, or do other slight time adjustments, such as performing the spell at dawn rather than later in the morning. Also, note that the new and full moons include not just the night of the astronomical new and full moons, but for the whole time the moon seems such; so a witch would consider it a new moon for the two or three nights where the moon cannot be seen in the sky, and would consider it a full moon for the three nights (and the days in between) or so where the moon looks completely round.

The New Moon

Traditionally, the new moon is not used to perform magic, as it is a time of rest and contemplation. This is a great time to meditate, contact spirits and ancestors, or do spiritual rather than purely magical work. This is the ideal time to write spells and get ingredients together, and make yourself emotionally ready to perform your new spells later during the lunar cycle. The last night of the new moon is an exception to this: the appearance of the new crescent moon is celebrated as a return of the moon from the dead, hence is the ideal time for new beginnings and starting long-term spells or projects—such as starting your herb garden!

The Waxing Moon

The waxing moon is the time to perform any magic that is designed to make things grow, such as gaining money or a promotion, or attracting love. This moon phase is sometimes called the right-handed moon, as the crescent looks like the shape made by your right thumb when pointing upward, and because positive/growing magic is done at this time. If you are having trouble keeping your herbs alive, you could do some positive magic now to help them.

The Full Moon

The full moon phase is governed by the Mother Goddess, and this is when the moon's power is at its strongest. It is a period of abundance and completion, so a time to put the finishing touches to a project, schedule a long-term spell to finish, or perform thanksgiving rituals and prayers for spells that have worked. A few minor spells are specifically designed to be performed at this time, but many witches use the full moon to work magic if they are unsure when to perform it—the strong, positive energy at this time will suit any spell. It's also a great time to do blessing spells and rituals, such as to bless a house, a new magical tool, or relationship—or indeed to consecrate your new Book of Shadows to write all your herbal spells in!

The Waning Moon

The waning moon is the time of sage wisdom, a time for crones. This moon phase is sometimes called the left-handed moon, as the crescent looks like the shape made by your left thumb when pointing upward, and because diminishing, or lessening, magic is done at this time. Good spells for this moon phase are spells to lose weight or decrease debt, to get rid of negative emotions or bad luck, and spells for protection. If you plan on asking your grandparents for local herbal lore, this would be a great time!

Actually writing the spell

Now, you get to actually write the spell. Hurray! I find it easiest to write spells like you would write a recipe: make a list of ingredients needed for the spell first, then name any pre-conditions (such as that the spell should be performed on a certain day of the week, or during a certain moon phase), then explain what to do during the actual spell work step by step. Try not to forget even the small steps, such as lighting a candle or how to use the herbs in the spell, and when to do so: it will make quite a difference to a spell whether a candle is lit throughout the spell, or whether it should be lit only at the end in order to burn something in it.

Similarly, explain what to do with any herbs listed in your ingredients: should the herb just sit on the altar, or be burnt? If they should be sprinkled around another object, such as a photo or candle, should this be done clockwise (to gain something/increase energy) or counter clockwise (to loose something/diminish energy)? If there is a vocal component to the spell, also write this down. Most spells with a vocal component rhyme: this is partially because it is tradition, but also because it is more pleasing to the ear to have rhymes, and it can help with the energy of the spell.

Spoken spells used to always rhyme because rhymes are easier to remember than long sentences. In the past, witchcraft was illegal, and thus it was dangerous to keep a written Book of Shadows. All spells were handed down from High Priestess to coven members orally.

But the words of your spell don't need to rhyme if you do not want them to. If you do have a vocal component to your spell, think carefully about the wording: even if you are angry about a bully, don't use curse words in your protection spell as it will only reflect badly on you. Also consider putting a caveat in there, to protect yourself and the target of your spell from any unintentional egotistical feelings and wrong intentions in the spell. A caveat may be something like the traditional "As above, so below," which is basically asking for the universe to provide balance with the spell, or "If it not be for the good of all, I wish this spell to fall." At the

"Monday for wealth
Tuesday for health
Wednesday the best day of all
Thursday for losses
Friday for crosses
And Saturday no luck at all."
Medieval rhyme

end of your chant or at the end of the spell, you may also want to include a power word or sentence, to seal your spell and send it out into the universe to work its magic. The traditional wording for that is "As I will it, so mote it be!" or:

"By the power of the moon
This magic will work soon
By the power of the sun
This spell's begun!"

However, you could say something as simple as "Now!" An easy way to combine your caveat and the power sentence is to say: "For the good of all, and the harm of none, this spell be done!"

When writing a herbal spell, keep in mind you might harm the herb! It's ok to harvest some of a herb—that is what they are for—but don't take so much of your herb that it damages the plant and it dies. When gathering a wild herb, keep in mind other witches and herbalists who might want some of the plant too.

Final touches

Once you have the spell worked out, go over it again with moral and ethical considerations in mind:

- Are your motives pure, and the magic "white", i.e., might the spell break the free will of anyone? Are you sure the spell will not harm you or anyone else, even unintentionally?
- When examining your spell to see if it harms anyone, don't just think of yourself and the person targeted with the spell! Your spell could harm others you don't think are involved at all, such as if the spell involves burying a witch bottle in the ground away from home, and the bottle ends up getting broken, and dug up by a child who cuts themselves on it.

If you are not sure about how pure your motives are in writing and performing a spell, consider using a divinatory tool to find out: for example, when I write a new spell, I usually consult my tarot cards about the spell's ingredients, its intentions and its likely outcome.

Keeping Track of Spells

In the old days, witches had a big grimoire, or Book of Shadows. This was essentially a notebook in which a witch would write down the spells they did, how they worked, and any modifications, etc. Often, after a new member was initiated in a coven, he or she was then given access to the High Priestess' Book of Shadows and expected to copy selected parts or maybe all of it, by hand. It was considered a great honor to be given access to all the spells and so much handed-down knowledge, and ensured that the new coven member had a good basis on which to build their own grimoire. Many witches these days still have something like it, because there is something very special, and very spiritual, to writing your own spells in your own hand into a big book. Plus you can get some very pretty leather-bound grimoires, or even create your own with handmade paper and a little padlock to keep it safe. You can even choose an ink color suitable to the spell to write it down, such as writing your health spells with a blue pen, your love spells in a red crayon, (or dragon's blood ink!) and so on.

MAGICAL INK

INGREDIENTS

- 3 CUPS VODKA OR PURE ALCOHOL
- 3 TABLESPOONS COFFEE GROUNDS
- 2 TABLESPOONS OF CINNAMON
- 1 TEASPOON OF GROUND CLOVES
- 5 CAMPHOR SEEDS AND SOME FRANKINCENSE GRANULES (BOTH OPTIONAL)

A simple magical ink you can make for writing into your Book of Shadows.

PREPARATION

Mix everything together in an airtight container and shake every day at dawn and dusk for two weeks. Then drain off the sediments and you'll have your magical ink! This ink will be brownish; you can use a colored liquor such as blue curacao or red wine if you want a specific color.

If you have an electronic Book of Shadows, keep your computer from crashing by placing an amethyst on top of it. But also make sure you back up your files regularly—you might even consider an online backup, such as Google Documents.

If you choose to have a paper Book of Shadows, I would strongly recommend writing your new spell down on a loose piece of paper or in a spiral notebook first. That way you can make changes if after the first time you perform the spell you feel it should be done on a different day of the week, or that a different herb should be used. These days, one does not need to fear persecution for performing spells, but if there are some personal spells you'd like to keep secret, you could write them in lemon juice or disguise the spell by writing it in a different language if you know any.

Of course, we live in the modern world and one of the great things about witchcraft is that it seamlessly integrates tradition and ancient wisdom with modern knowledge and abilities. So, many witches keep their Book of Shadows on their computer these days. It makes it easier to change spells when you find a mistake, share your magic with coven members or online friends, and it also makes searching for that particular banishing spell or ancestor ritual easier. If you choose to have an electronic Book of Shadows, you should protect it from prying eyes by using a password, even if you are the only one using that computer—this will not only protect your privacy and the spells you worked so hard to create, but will also stop misunderstandings with people who might read a spell that could look odd or like black magic when taken out of context. Having your Book of Shadows on the computer also means you can add notes as you go along—every time you perform a spell, write down the details of when you performed it, the moon phase, where you got the herb from you used, any special circumstances (even small stuff such as the phone rang during the spell and while you didn't answer it, it distracted you, or a bird flew to your windowsill just as you blew out the candle, etc). A lunar cycle after you performed the spell, go back and note the results of the spell, if any—you can do this earlier if you get results earlier, and of course you can also go back later if the spell takes a while to work and you only see results after a few months. But most spells take less than a month to work if they are going to work, so one lunar cycle is a good guide to check for results.

Tables of Magical Associations

COLORS AND THEIR MAGICAL CORRESPONDENCES	Pink	Red	Dark red	Light green	Dark green	Pale brown	Brown	Gold	White
Primary magic	Love	Sex	Warding	Changing attitudes	Prosperity	Travel	Work	Money	Peace
Secondary magic	Harmony	Passion	Vigor	Weather	Fertility	Building	Animals	Beauty	Purification
Herb	Red clover	Chili	Red	Feverfew	Irish moss	Ginger	Mandrake	Pennyroyal	Camomile

HERBS AND SPELL INTENT	Love	Sex	Fertility	Work	Money	Protection	Friendship	Curse-breaking	Luck
Primary herb	Cinnamon	Red peppercorn	Mandrake	Irish moss	Basil	Clove	Valerian	Bergamot	Nutmeg
Secondary herb	Jasmine	Chili	Patchouli	Thyme	Pennyroyal	Mustard	Cardamom	Wild garlic	Red clover
Crystal	Rose quartz	Garnet	Emerald	Tiger's eye	Malachite	Amethyst	Amber	Onyx	Obsidian
Color	Pink	Red	Green	Brown	Gold	White	Yellow	Black	Silver
God	Eros	Pan	Amun	Lugh	Ra	Atlas	Baldr	Osiris	Odin
Goddess	Aphrodite	Venus	Cerridwen	Demeter	Oshun	Artemis	Hestia	Persephone	Athena

THE ELEMENTS AND THEIR MAGICAL CORRESPONDENCES	Earth	Air	Fire	Water
Direction	North	East	South	West
Color	Brown	Yellow	Red	Blue
Crystal	Tiger's eye	Diamond	Opal	Aquamarine
Magical tool	Pentagram	Wand	Athame	Chalice
Season	Fall	Spring	Summer	Winter
Animal	Stag	Birds	Salamander	Fish
Altar symbol	Salt	Incense	Candle	Water
Time of day	Morning	Dawn	Noon	Night
God	Cernunnos	Toth	Loki	Poseidon
Goddess	Demeter	Arianrhod	Brigit	Venelia
Magic	Inner strength	Intuition	Energy	Cleansing

Yellow	Black	Silver	Orange	Blue	Dark blue	Gray	Purple	Lavender
Friendship	Curse-breaking	Luck	Justice	Health	Confidence	Ancestors	Occult knowledge	Psychic awareness
Exams	Protection	Gambling	Leadership	Home	Wisdom protection	Patience	Power	Blessing
Citronella	Black	Eyebright	Oregano	Rosemary	Thistle	Sage	Chives	Lavender

Justice	Health	Confidence	Fairies	Ancestors
Verveine	Camomile	Tarragon	Thistle	Lemon balm
Dill	Feverfew	Marjoram	Juniper	Rue
Topaz	Turquoise	Clear quartz	Moonstone	Hematite
Orange	Blue	Dark blue	Rainbow	Gray
Forseti	Apollo	Zeus	Loki	Anubis
Maat	Brigit	Isis	Morrigan	Arianrhod

HERBS AND DAYS OF THE WEEK

	Monday	Tuesday	Wednesday	Thursday	Friday	Saturday	Sunday
Herb	Fennel	Chili	Eyebright	Basil	Cinnamon	Clove	Star anise
Magic	Healing	Power	Divination	Money	Love	Protection	Happiness
Deity	Moon	Mars	Mercury	Jupiter	Venus	Saturn	Sun
Color	Silver	Red	Purple	Blue	Pink	Gray	Gold
Crystal	Opal	Ruby	Amethyst	Sapphire	Rose quartz	Quartz crystal	Carnelian

Glossary

ATHAME A ritual knife that is not used to cut things physically, but for magic and working with energy, such as dipping the tip of the blade in a bowl of herbs on the altar to charge them with magical energy for future use in spells or medicinal teas. Traditionally has a black handle.

ASTRAL PLANE A different plane of existence from that inhabited by humans, said to be where spirits live.

BESOM WITCH'S BROOM Often decorated with cleansing herbs, such as sage, parsley, and rosemary to symbolically cleanse the ritual space before working magic, or decorated with herbs and flowers to look pretty for a handfasting.

BOLLINE Knife used to cut things used for magic such as herbs or cord. Traditionally has a white handle.

BOOK OF SHADOWS A diary for a witch to write down spells and magic; often kept online these days. Abbreviated to BoS.

CAULDRON A large pot or bowl, traditionally black, used to make magical foods and for water-scrying.

CLEANSING Spiritual cleaning, removing negativity.

COVEN A group of witches working magic together regularly.

DEOSIL Clockwise direction.

DIVINATION Reading the future with tarot cards, runes, or other methods.

ESBAT Coven meeting, usually on a full moon.

FAMILIAR Animal, often a pet, who helps in magic.

GRIMOIRE See Book of Shadows.

GROUNDING Releasing excess energy after magic.

HANDFASTING Wiccan wedding.

HIGHPRIEST/ESS Coven leader and teacher.

JOSS STICK Incense in stick form, usually bought rather than homemade.

OINTMENT A medical semi-solid preparation used to soothe the head or skin.

PAGAN Originally any believer in non-monotheistic religion, but these days usually means a believer in earth-based spirituality (Wiccan, Druid, Shaman, etc).

PANTHEON A group of deities associated with a particular culture, such as the Celtic pantheon or Greek pantheon.

PATRON DEITY A deity you feel especially close to.

PENTACLE A five-pointed star in a circle; sometimes a five-petalled flower is used to symbolize this on the altar, or a pentagram made from stalks of herbs.

PENTAGRAM A five-pointed star without a circle; although often used interchangeably with pentacle.

PSYCHIC A person who is extremely sensitive to energies and otherwordly entities.

REDE/WICCAN REDE The basic Wiccan moral standpoint: "And it harm none, do as thou wilt."

SABBAT MAJOR Wiccan festival. There are eight each year, beginning with October 31 and Samhain, through Yule, Imbolc, Ostara, Beltane, Litha, Lammas, and Mabon.

SALVE See ointment.

SCRYING Form of divination done by looking in a pool of water, crystal ball, mirror, etc.

SYGIL A magical symbol, often personally designed.

SKYCLAD Naked for the purpose of ritual magic.

TALISMAN A magical amulet.

VISUALIZATION Imagining something in your mind's eye. Also used for very deep meditation.

WARDING Protecting something magically.

WIDDERSHINS Anticlockwise.

Resources

Websites

www.thealmanack.com
A calendar-style website which gives you the current moon phases, planets that rule certain days, etc. Has a handy monthly printable page.

www.botanical.com
Great online herbal encyclopedia.

www.paganfed.org (The Pagan Federation)
www.witchcraft.org (Children of Artemis)
Two UK-based Pagan organizations.

www.aquariantabernaclechurch.org
Great American Wiccan website.

www.sacred-texts.com
Lots of religious and spiritual texts here, including Wicca, Pagan, Druid, and Witchcraft.

www.facebook.com/SiljasGreenWiccan
My Facebook page, regularly updated with news and other links of interest.

Bibliography

Cunningham's Encyclopedia of Magical Herbs Scott Cunningham (Llewellyn Publications, Woodbury, USA, 2000). Great reference for herbs and their magical meanings.

Culpeper's Complete Herbal Nicholas Gent Culpeper (Wordsworth Editions Ltd, London, 2007). A reprint of the original seventeenth-century publication.

The Biodynamic Year Maria Thun and Matthew Barton (Temple Lodge Publishing, East Sussex, 2007). Planting by the moon and the influence of planets.

The Complete Book of Essential Oils and Aromatherapy Valerie Ann Worwood (New World Library, Novato, USA, 1991). Lists more than 500 oils and tons of recipes using essential oils as alternatives to human-made health, beauty, and cleaning products.

Sacred Plant Medicine: The Wisdom in Native American Herbalism Stephen Harrod Buhner (RobertsRinehart Publishers, Boulder, USA and Dublin, Ireland, 1996). Lists medicinal uses of herbs and ceremonial elements such as prayers and medicine songs associated with their use.

Last Child in the Woods Richard Louv (Algonquin Books, Chapel Hill, USA, 2008). A book encouraging us to teach our kids about nature, and let them run free every now and then.

Herbs: Organic Gardening Basics Organic Gardening Magazine (Rodale Books, Emmaus, USA, 2001). Shows you how to plan a practical herb garden, harvest at the right time, and provide the best care without using chemicals.

Index

Bold pagination shows main entry

Air 50–56, 80–81, 154
alfalfa **78**
allspice **51**, 116, 129, 138
almond 11, **80**, 100, 117, 139
animal magic 54, 68, 72, 142
anxiety 54, 57, 60, 73, 84, 117
apple 13, 99
astral projection 55, 71

bad behavior spell 112
bad habits 15, 70
banishing spells 45, 50, 51
basil **66**; beauty recipes 137, 138; growing 33, 34, 35, 38; in the home 140, 141; sleep tea 136; spells using 26, 34, 89, 90, 93, 94, 108
baths 56, 62, 70, 73, 97, 116, 117, 137
bay 26, **63**, 89, 93, 107, 108, 120
beauty recipes 72, 137–139
bergamot **59**, 96, 131
black magic 11, 115, 153
blackberry **78**
blessing oil 122, 127, 139, 149
blueberry **80**
body spells 116, 121
Book of Shadows 39, 44, 46, 71, 149, 152–153
buckthorn **68**, 109

camomile 13, 34, 42, **69**, 90, 116, 130, 135, 139, 141
camphor 19, **75**, 143, 152
candle magic **10**, **14**, 92, 96, 99, 103, 109, 111, 112, 113, 116, 121, 123
candy, cinnamon 132
caraway seed **55**, 121, 135
cardamom **53**, 90, 97, 104, 105
catnip 38, 39, **72**, 138, 142
celery **84**
charm bags 16
chastity 84
cheese, herb 131
children 51, 62, 82, 133
chili 19, 34, 46, 47, **61**, 101, 132, 143
chives 15, **70**, 128, 131
Christianity 27
cinnamon **61**; beauty recipes 138; in food/drink 129, 132; magical ink 152; spells using 92, 96, 100, 101, 108, 127
circle, casting 19, 65
circulation 58, 63, 65, 67, 75, 84
citronella 14, **60**, 107, 134, 138, 139, 141, 143
cleansing 54, 56, 58, 65, 83, 131
clover, red 13, **74**, 89, 107, 108, 132, 133, 134
cloves 31, **64**, 104, 112, 129, 138, 140, 141, 152
colds/coughs 50, 56, 57, 59, 70, 71, 74, 83, 135
color 10, 14, 35, 36, 147, 154
concentration 74, 84, 85, 127
confidence 36, 52, 63, 122, 137
copper coins 84, 90, 92
cord magic 15
corn **82**
courage 71, 72
covens 12, 19, 32, 54, 152
crystals 16, 107, 153, 154
cucumber **84**
culinary uses 6, 13, 125, 128–136
Culpeper 23–24
cumin 26, **50**, 113, 122, 123, 139
curses 50, 56, 59, 64, 129

days of week 32, 155
deities 10, 14, 17, 19, 32, 33, 43, 49
departed, contacting 35, 58, 83, 123, 149
depression 55, 68, 72, 73
digestion: drinks for 133, 135; foods for 81, 82, 83, 85; herbs for 34, 50, 51, 54, 55, 59, 60, 62, 64, 65, 66, 71
dill **62**, 111, 133
Dioscorides 22–23
divination 53, 58, 81, 85, 151
dragon magic 16, 52
dream magic 17, 70, 73, 85, 123
dreams 65, 68, 70, 81
drink 13, 19, 34, 126–127, 133–136

Earth 50–55, 78–79, 154
East 50–56, 80–81
eggs 35, 132
elder 47, 130, 134, 136
elements 19, 48, 49, 154
energy: of herbs 29, 32, 35, 36, 38, 40, 41, 45, 46; raising 19, 60, 62
Esbats 12, 32
essential oils 14, 15, 23, 42–43, 49, 126
ethics 11, 151
eucalyptus **70**, 113, 138, 148
exams/studying 55, 74, 84, 85, 118, 127
eyebright 19, **58**, 111

fairy magic 16, 43, 65, 67, 72
fennel 26, 34, **71**, 101, 128, 133, 135, 137